OH SHIT!
IT'S JESUS!
the relevance of Jesus without all the religious crap

STEVE HUGHES

ISBN: 1-4196-8640-2
ISBN-13: 9781419686405

Visit www.booksurge.com to order additional copies.

Dedication

This book is dedicated to all my friends who have journeyed with me through life in Yosemite National Park.

What's Inside

Introduction

Wow, or "Oh Shit!" you are actually sitting down and reading this book! As a confessed workaholic I know how valuable your time is. There may be a time after a really long day that you feel confused about where the heck everything is headed in your life and our world. I hope that the events in Jesus' life we'll discuss will prompt some transparent reflection in your life. I hope that the topics addressed find some resonance within you. Through this introspection, I hope you will find the reality that God desires to be in your life.

Stereotypes suck! Labeling people is something that at times we can't keep out of our heads. That being the case, how would you identify or describe your spiritual beliefs? As you think about this, try to avoid loaded generic terms or labels (like God, Agnostic, and Christian) to explain who you are spiritually. Go ahead take some time to think about what you believe and how those beliefs truly affect, or have little to no affect, on your life.....

I'll wait.......(*I'll go inspect my climbing webbing.....*)

Thanks for coming back! I hope that was beneficial.

Concerning stereotypes, who do you think I am based upon the title of this book? You may think I'm a former (or current) "pot smoking – liberal – hippie – angry with God" guy. I'm none of those. I've never smoked pot, but I do like my rock-nroll. Growing up, I helped my Granddad vaccinate cattle and hauled square bales of hay with my brothers, good memories. My older brother and I would go to the beach to surf and skim board. I've had a personal connection with God since I was a teenager. I graduated from Texas A&M University with a Bachelor of Science degree *(If you're ever in Aggieland, drive west to the town of Caldwell, find a bakery and ask for a Kolache – Czech heaven!)*

Now just with that little bit of personal information some of you will form opinions about my philosophical and theological viewpoints. What I'm asking of you is to sincerely have an open mind about God, myself, and others. You really don't know someone until you hang out with them in various settings and situations and see how they live. The same is true with Jesus. In the pages ahead you'll be able to hang out with Jesus.

Words have meaning and these meanings are often very subjective in nature. I'm sure that some of my words in this book will be misunderstood. If you have any questions about what is written please contact me at steve@ohshititsjesus.com. My hope is that you will know more about the person and message of Jesus by the end of this book than you do now.

Despite the title of this book, cursing and profanity are not a normal part of my speech. However, as Jesus lived out his everyday life and talked with others people had very strong responses. One reaction was from the religious leaders. They were the pastors and priests of the church of the day. These were so-called "men of God" who were respected and had power in the community.

Jesus was a homeless wandering spiritual teacher, with no formal education. His teaching was attracting a popular following among the people, men and women. Jesus' teachings were at times in direct opposition to the cultural religious leaders. He called them out when they were being unjust, selfish, and prideful. As Jesus walked up the stone steps of the Temple in Jerusalem in sandals, his feet covered in dirt, the priests would see him coming and without a doubt would shake their heads and say, "Oh shit! It's Jesus!"

Most of the priests and religious leaders in Jesus' time misunderstood him spiritually. They saw his teachings as a threat to their power in society, and his moral goodness exposed their selfish and hypocritical lifestyles. That same reaction still occurs today, but for somewhat different reasons. Reasons we'll explore in more depth later. So what about you? When you hypothetically, "see Jesus coming" how do you react? You may shake your head and say, "Oh shit! It's Jesus!"

In Jesus' time there were many people who were searching for something different than what the cultural church of the day offered. Jesus was different. He accepted people on the margins; people who weren't goody-goodies. A friend of one of my friends decided to become a follower of Christ. He was extremely excited about his new relationship, and, as a man with many tattoos, the first thing he did was to go get some fresh ink. On his bicep, in dark black ink, blazed "Jesus is the Shit." He meant it with every fiber of his being. The people who hung out with Jesus were a little rough around the edges. Out of loving expectation they would see Jesus coming and literally say with joy "Oh shit! It's Jesus!" In the pages ahead we'll be looking at people's lives now and twenty centuries in the past. We'll be talking about different life issues and we'll discover that when people see Jesus coming they will say in either a negative or positive mindset, "Oh, shit! It's Jesus!" I hope that at some point in the future you'll also be able to say with joy, "Oh shit! It's Jesus!"

Within each chapter you will find a "Jesus Story." These are the actual day-to-day walking around experiences that Jesus had with his friends and enemies. I have paraphrased these events so they can be better understood and therefore more relevant and applicable to our own journey with God.

Chapter One
I Know Other Christians,
but You're Different

Have you been to Hawaii? Pacific paradise, right? I'm in Hawaii now, my second visit. Of course, I can only afford to come to Hawaii when someone else pays my way. I'm speaking at a ministry conference. This morning, at 5:30, I went running along the Waikiki beachfront. A full moon sent moonlight splashing across the ocean and waves, paradise.

In Hawaii, like other places with good weather, there are, sadly, numerous homeless people. During my run, I saw a bundle that looked like clothing and a pack lying on a bench facing the ocean. I thought, "This looks like a homeless person's belongings, but where is the homeless person?"

At the halfway point of my run right before the sun rose out of the ocean I saw pastel colored clouds in front of a glowing morning sky, paradise. Running back along the beachfront I smelled marijuana coming from the ocean side park, it's now 6:30 a.m. I run past the bench again with the bundle on it. In the increasing morning light I realize that the "bundle" I saw earlier was in fact a woman, a "daughter of Eve", Paradise?

That night my wife and I had dinner at a restaurant overlooking the ocean and the setting sun, paradise. Walking back to our hotel room, my wife and I saw a young woman in obvious distress.

She was sobbing, bent over with her hands to her face. Something had caused her great pain and grief. There were people around her who seemed to be friends or family. My heart wanted to stop and try to help and comfort her in some way, paradise?

In this day, I saw the hopelessness of a homeless woman curled up on a park bench, the emptiness of a young man getting high overlooking one of the most beautiful scenes on earth, and a young woman crying in deep personal pain. There is real life even in paradise. Followers of Christ should actively respond to the situations of tragedy and pain found in our communities. In what real and substantial way can Jesus and His followers do to help these people?

How the "church" responds to people in need determines in some measure how American society perceives Jesus and how individuals respond to Jesus. Unfortunately, many people only experience hypocrisy and hatred coming from the church.

Some, maybe you, think of Christians as people who are part of the "right-wing conservative hate group" or an archaic organized religion imposing their unrealistic morality upon society. We could discuss those issues and I would actually love to, but now I want you to know that many Christians and churches are not like that. They are responding to situations of pain and tragedy by loving and serving people like Jesus did. They care about the community of humanity, the personal struggles of individuals, and provide substantive assistance to their neighbors.

Individual followers of Christ can be like Jesus and love those who are not loved by others in a society. There are numerous examples of this in Christian history - Saint Patrick in Ireland, Father Damien on a Hawaiian leper island, and Mother Teresa in Calcutta to name a few. When you see people love and care for one another, you are actually catching a glimpse of Jesus.

If you don't accept or understand the whole Jesus thing right now, I hope that you can become friends with a follower of Christ who is striving to be like Jesus. In doing so you can catch a glimpse of and even touch the invisible and intangible God that Jesus followers trust their lives to. Being like Jesus is what makes followers of Christ different from the Christians you know.

If you're not a Christian, you may have had some negative experiences with Christians. They may have tried to convert you and slammed you with Bible verses about how "evil and sinful" you are. You may have seen media accounts of so-called "Christians" protesting and shouting ugly slurs against homosexuals or other groups.

You may be dechurched. You attended church at one time, but then someone said or did something hurtful. We avoid pain, so you left the church. It saddens me if that has been your only exposure to the church or Christians.

The local group of Christ Followers that I'm a part of is called the "Tribe of Jesus." In the first century, a Roman historian, Flavius Josephus was writing about Israel and the Jewish people. He wrote about a teacher, Jesus, who was reported performing miracles, and it was even said by many that he rose from the dead and came back to life. The people who followed Jesus' teachings and believed in his resurrection were identified by Josephus as the Tribe of Christians. Since the term Christian has lost most of its positive meaning, we call ourselves the Tribe of Jesus.

In our local Tribe of Jesus, we strive to do our best at following God's commands to be humble, forgiving, and loving toward everyone. As a Tribe, we depend on each other for our spiritual and personal well-being. It's reassuring when a friend tells someone in our Tribe, "You're different from the other Christians I know. The Christians I know don't seem to be real or have an authentic personal spiritual life but you do." At times we hear, "The Christians I know live somewhat like me and my friends. They get drunk, sleep with whoever they're seeing, and have a casual attitude about their spirituality. But you don't do those things. You aren't judgmental. You're serious about your beliefs and cool to be around." We want to be like Jesus and Jesus was different. He was not the typical Rabbi (Hebrew word for teacher) and spiritual leader.

zzz

Jesus Story

During the religious culture of Jesus' day it was a big deal in the community when a local religious leader invited a visiting spiritual teacher to his house to discuss moral and spiritual issues. The established religious leaders could not ignore Jesus. His revolutionary teachings about loving your enemies and God's love for everyone regardless of "who and what" they were appealed to many. There were thousands of witnesses to Jesus' miraculous acts; they had seen him supernaturally create food to feed thousands of people. Jesus healed those physically blind from birth to new sight, and he even brought the dead back to life. Jesus' teachings and miracles caused many to wonder, "Who is this miracle worker and religious rebel and what is he trying to accomplish?"

Jesus was travelling around the villages in the Galilee area. An important religious leader, Simon, invited him to come speak and teach at his home. As the news spread through the town that Jesus would speak, the invited and uninvited began to arrive at the home of the well-to-do Simon. The invited important guests and other religious leaders arrived at the home and sat on the floor leaning against a low banquet table. The guests would lean on one arm, eat with the other, and have their feet pointed away from the table. The uninvited people were allowed to come into the home as long as they were quiet and stayed a distance away from the banquet table and the invited religious leaders.

By having many people in his home to hear an important teacher, Simon would increase his standing in the community. The men were situated around the table eating and listening to Jesus teach. Simon and the other religious leaders basked in this public exposure and their assumed authority to discern Jesus' relevancy for the community. From the edge of the crowd a beautiful woman appeared and approached the banquet table. Immediately the crowd and the religious leaders were taken aback by her lack of social protocol, especially since they knew "who and what" she was.

First, she was a woman approaching this man's only banquet table. Her head and hair were uncovered, which meant she was probably a prostitute, according to their local customs. Everyone in the community knew her as an immoral woman who slept around. She was shunned and hated by the religious in town. As she walked around the table past the religious leaders they each scooted closer to the table, away from her, hoping not to be contaminated by her presence. She humbly knelt down at Jesus' feet. Every eye in the house was upon her as murmurs and harsh whispers filled the air. She blocked all that out. She was on a journey of renewal and overwhelming gratitude.

She laid an expensive bottle of perfume on the ground as she knelt. The emotions swelled up from within her chest. Tears of joy and hope filled her eyes, overflowed, and ran down her face. Her tears began falling on Jesus' feet. She reached behind her neck, pulled her hair forward, and began cleaning and drying Jesus dirty dusty feet using her tears and hair. After his feet were clean she began kissing his feet and rubbing expensive perfume on them.

For the religious leaders and those in the house this was reprehensible! A prostitute, an unclean and immoral woman was touching and kissing the feet of a Rabbi! In their beliefs, Jesus was now unclean, spiritually unacceptable before God. The perfume itself was not sinful, but they knew she used this perfume in her business as a prostitute. In their minds, her rubbing this perfume on Jesus was a sinful act, tainting Jesus.

Simon didn't say anything out loud but in his head he thought "Well that's that! Jesus is definitely not a prophet sent by God. God would have clearly shown him that this woman is a sinner. Jesus should have nothing to do with her, especially letting her touch him." Jesus, being God, could hear the thoughts of Simon. So Jesus said, "Simon, I have a question for you." Simon still being polite says, "Yes Teacher, go ahead. What is it?"

Jesus told this story: "A loan officer loans money to two people, two months salary to one and two years' salary to the other. When it comes time to pay back the loan the two people are unable to pay back the money. Instead of having these guys arrested, thrown into prison and seizing their property (consequences by law back then), the loan officer kindly forgives these guys and cancels their debt to him. Which of the two men do you think loved the loan officer more?" Simon answered, "I assume the guy who owed the two years' salary?" Jesus said, "That's exactly right!"

Jesus looked at the woman kneeling at his feet and then, with intent, told Simon, "Look at this woman. Go ahead look at her. When I entered your house you didn't provide the usual and polite gesture of water to wash my dusty feet. However, this woman has lovingly washed my feet with her tears and dried them with her hair. You didn't even shake my hand or give me a kiss of greeting (something common even today in some cultures), but she has kissed my feet over and over again to show her respect and love for me. You didn't even offer me the common courtesy of olive oil for my head (used to heal dry skin). Yet this woman has anointed my feet with expensive perfume and kissed my feet over and over again."

Jesus continued, "I tell you; I know this woman has led an immoral life and has made many choices causing harm and destruction to her life and many other lives. Yet all of that is forgiven and forgotten because in her heart she desires God's love and has shown love to myself and God. A person who is forgiven little will only give back a little love." Jesus looked at the woman and said to her with love and assurance, "Your sins are forgiven."

This statement was the most shocking thing that had happened at the banquet so far! Only God can forgive sins! This woman had not gone to the Temple and offered a sacrifice for her sins, as required in the religious tradition of the day. Yet, Jesus had the *audacity to violate religious law and equate himself with the Almighty God!*

That was it! The religious leaders at the table were really pissed off now. They said out loud to each other, "Who the hell does this guy think he is?! You can't go around forgiving someone's sin!"

Knowing the tense nature of the moment and the growing hostility in the crowd, Jesus said to the woman personally and to everyone that could hear, "Your faith has saved you; go in peace." She stood up and felt like a completely new and different person in her heart and mind. She peacefully walked out of the house, a new person.

– Jesus Story paraphrased from Luke 7:36-50

⌘ ⌘ ⌘

You may know a cultural or organized religion version of Jesus. There is a Jesus that is different from the "Jesus" you may have heard about or seen.

Now how about the Christians you know? Do they resemble the legalism and attitude of Simon and the other religious leaders? Do the Christians you know reflect the love and forgiveness Jesus expressed? Do the Christians you know exhibit the changed joyous and humble life before a loving God like the woman in this story? There are Christians, followers of Christ, who are different from what you have personally seen or heard.

Do Something

Why was Jesus, a poor day laborer given the honor to speak at this banquet? He was different. How did the immoral woman find forgiveness and new life outside of the organized religion of her day? Through Jesus, He was different. He was God. Where can you find the real and relevant life found in God? You can start by forgiving someone – really! Who this week or years ago cut you off on the freeway or said something hurtful to you? Forgive them. Let the bitterness and anger begin to slide away. Understand how much God loves and forgives you for the times you're a pain in the ass! Be forgiving, you'll be amazed at how it will change your life.

Please send your critical comments, encouragements, and questions to steve@ohshititsjesus.com. You can post your thoughts and join a discussion about the book and this chapter on www.ohshititsjesus.com and on the Facebook group "Oh Shit Its Jesus."

Chapter Two
Street Preachers, Jesus Freaks, Bible Thumpers, & Other Annoying People

Telemarketers, spam email, and pop-up internet ads. What emotion did I just evoke with those words? You can stop cursing now. Why are telemarketers, spam email, & pop-up internet ads so annoying? Could one reason be that they're uninvited intrusions into your personal space? Kind of like the weird feeling you get when someone talks too close to you and invades your personal space. You want to just politely back away and end the conversation as soon as possible.

Street preachers, Jesus freaks, and Bible thumpers are uninvited intrusions into our spiritual personal space. Like at your home, you invite people in that you know, trust, and have an interest in. The same is true for our spiritual personal space. You only invite in those beliefs and people that you know, choose to trust, and have an interest in.

How is that personal knowledge, trust, and interest acquired? It usually happens through a relationshipbasedonfamiliarity,sharedexperiences, relevance, reliability and faith in someone. Most street preachers, Jesus freaks, and Bible thumpers offer blind trust, intellectual dishonesty, unrealistic expectations, and legalism. They may have good intentions, but they do not offer an interesting view of what Jesus was all about.

Sometimes when you're at the grocery store, you'll try a completely new item like tofu with a spicy sausage flavoring, yumm!! (It's actually very good). The reason you may choose this new item is because it may fit a need or interest you currently have. It may also be creatively marketed and packaged to catch your attention. Many street preachers, Jesus freaks, and Bible thumpers, do not fill a personal spiritual need and they could win an award for negative marketing and packaging! Another reason that street preachers, Jesus freaks, and Bible thumpers are annoying is that they are trying to "sell" you something you don't need or want. Jesus is not "something" to be sold, marketed, or packaged. Jesus is someone to be known.

Think about either a hobby or cause you're deeply involved in now. How did you first get involved in that? Did your parents or friends introduce you to it? Was it something that just randomly caught your attention, and you pursued it? Whatever you do and are involved in is by your choice. You don't go skydiving for the first time because someone has won a debate with you. You skydive because you make the choice. You don't volunteer each week with the at-risk kids because a stranger has told you that you're a horrible person and that you should feel guilty for not helping the kids. You volunteer because you care about people and community.

Christ followers who are on a journey with Jesus do so because we choose to do so. We do not follow Jesus because he is fire insurance from Hell. We follow Jesus because he was and is a real person that we have come to know and love. Jesus is someone to have a shared personal experience with. Jesus is someone you yourself personally choose to include in your spiritual zone of comfort.

It's important to know that Jesus is not a cause or a hobby. However, some who attend church make Jesus just that in their life. As Christ Followers, we believe Jesus was and is God. We strive to learn and apply the teachings of Jesus into our lives and allow the Spirit of Jesus to make us better people. As someone focused on the good in life, God can use us to help make our community and world a positive, nurturing, and loving place. Because we believe Jesus is God, we never want to be separated from him, now or for eternity. Jesus promises everyone that if you believe in him and have faith in him like a child, he adopts you into his spiritual family.

Jesus has invited you into his house, to be a part of his Tribe and community. That invitation is open to everyone, everywhere! That's a huge invitation! Think about the invitations that you accept or reject. You accept invitations from people you trust, people you have developed a relationship with and people who care for you. I hope you can have a friendship with a Christ Follower who is on a trusting journey with Jesus. I hope you will begin to know Jesus, trust in what he taught, and in time, accept Jesus' invitation to know his love.

God has been giving this invitation to humans forever. However, as with any good thing that God gives us, we can totally screw it up at times. Next is a Jesus story that talks about that.

⌘ ⌘ ⌘

Jesus Story

In the first year that Jesus started teaching and healing people, he went to Jerusalem for the Passover Celebration. Jesus, as a Jewish boy, had been to the Temple for the Passover Celebration pretty much every year of his life. It was a huge holiday event in Jerusalem with people coming in from all over the Roman Empire. Passover celebrated the Hebrews escape from slavery in Egypt through God's power and it celebrated their freedom to pursue God's purpose in their daily lives.

During the holiday week, the Temple was the epicenter of the social and religious activities. People would come to worship God at the Temple. They offered up animal sacrifices to God so their sins would be forgiven and their spiritual standing with God would be okay.

Let me explain "animal sacrifices" here. Ancient Israel was an agrarian society. The vast majority of the people farmed and raised livestock. How well your crops and livestock did each year was a serious life and death issue for your family. Your crops and livestock provided an income and the food needed to live. This is a real life scenario totally unfamiliar to Americans today.

The original intent of the sacrifice was to bring your best animal and offer it as a significant gift to God. The animal sacrifice meant less money, less food, and a less secure well-being for your family. Sacrificing your best milking goat meant trusting God to provide for you and your family's needs. The sacrifice was meant to be a heart felt desire to honor the God of the universe with your best. Why honor him? Because God loves and cares for you more than anything else that He has created. Plus, God created and gave you the goat in the first place. This original intent and personal meaning of the sacrifice had been lost and corrupted because of the organized religion in Jesus' day. Similarly, today's organized religion has in many ways, devalued Jesus' message of trusting him with your life.

Jesus went to the Temple and knew what to expect, He had seen it his whole life, but now he had a mission. There were merchants in the Temple that sold animals to be used as sacrifices in the Temple. Just like today, some people are always looking for the easy way out. Most people thought that traveling to Jerusalem with their sacrificial animals was too much of a burden. Why sacrifice your best milk goat when you can buy a sheep, worth a whole lot less, and have it sacrificed instead? If you were rich and considered yourself important, you could buy a more expensive animal and offer up a better sacrifice to impress others. The hypocrisy, legalism, and insincerity were repulsive to God and Jesus.

As if that hypocrisy was not bad enough, consider what else was going on at the Temple. Using a current day example let's say you go to a church service to connect with God, ask His forgiveness, and to renew the personal faith and comfort you have in knowing God. You show up and they say that only people who are Canadians are allowed in the main sanctuary to worship. Everyone else, Americans, Kiwis, and Texans are directed to a smaller side room to worship.

But that's not all. In this smaller worship room, there are people selling the wine and bread you need to participate in the Lord's Supper. The Lord's Supper is a time when Christians celebrate Jesus' love for them. This love was shown in Jesus' decision to die as a sacrifice for the arrogance people have towards God and their inherent nature to have destructive actions and thoughts. The bread and wine symbolically represent Jesus' body and blood that was respectively crucified and shed for our benefit.

In the small worship room for non-Canadians, the sellers are loud, trying to attract your attention because they are competing with each other. However, after getting your attention they won't take your American cash and coins. They will only take Canadian currency. There are other merchants who are money exchangers so that you can obtain the needed Canadian money to take the Lord's Supper. You exchange your money but you're totally getting ripped off. The merchants give you only 50 cents of Canadian money for every American dollar you give them. Oh, and the church leaders are getting a cut on the American money being exchanged and lining their pockets. They drive around in their luxury sedans with a Jesus Fish decal on the back and a bumper sticker that says "You'll wish you had Jesus stickers on your car on Judgment Day". After all this crap, how are you supposed to get into a worshipful attitude with all the noise, disrespect for God, and corruption going on?

Now's the correct time to ask, "What Would Jesus Do?" if he showed up at this church? Well, we know exactly what He did at the Temple. He was so angry he found some rope and made it into a whip. He began cracking the whip and yelling at the merchants, "Get out of my Father's house! How dare you turn this place of worship into a place of greed and mockery?" These people were uninvited intrusions into the personal space of God and His children. When Jesus started chasing everyone out, some of the religious leaders heard the commotion and cursed, "Oh shit! It's Jesus!"

Jesus chases out the merchants and animals. He was throwing and kicking over their tables, spilling their money all over the filthy floor. The Americans, Kiwis, and Texans would be thinking, "Yes! It's about time someone kicked some butt and dealt with this!"

After Jesus had done his thing, the Temple leaders came and confronted Jesus. They adamantly demanded, "Who do you think you are? If you think you have the authority from God to do this, then perform some miracle for us to prove it!"

Jesus catching his breath said, "All right". Jesus slowly looked around and said, "Completely tear down and destroy this Temple and I'll raise it back up in three days." The Temple leaders laughed and shot back, "What! We've been remodeling and expanding this Temple for forty-six years! You're going to bring it down and rebuild it in three days?" Jesus knew that the Temple was just a building, it was not the true dwelling place of God. It had nothing to do with the reality of God's presence in a person's life. Jesus was in fact God. His body the actual indwelling of God. What he meant by destroying this Temple was a metaphor for his own bodily destruction by being crucified to death in a couple of years. The "three days" alludes to the three days Jesus would be dead after his crucifixion. "Raise it back up" refers to Jesus' resurrection from a brutal death. The Temple leaders had no idea what he was talking about. Later Jesus' followers remembered what he said and the importance of what he was teaching them at that moment.

– Jesus Story paraphrased from John 2:13-22.

⌘　⌘　⌘

Many of the leaders of the Temple had a misguided view of God, how to know Him, and what worshipping God meant. Today there are Christ Followers who understand and know the reality of having a relationship with God. I hope you can find one to talk with or find a church that realistically shares the message and love of Jesus. They're out there. You have to look a little harder to find them, but they exist. I hope that you desire the life that Jesus taught about and seek after a community of faith that strives to live out his message.

Do Something

If you know a Christian or a preacher type that presents a negative view of Jesus and the church, in a polite way tell them the reality about what they've done to push people away from listening to Jesus.

If you're a Christ Follower and you know of a Christian or church that does something that is insulting, damaging, clueless, insensitive, etc., please write, call, or talk to them please!

Please send your critical comments, encouragements, and questions to steve@ ohshititsjesus.com. You can post your thoughts and join a discussion about the book and this chapter on www.ohshititsjesus.com and on the Facebook group "Oh Shit Its Jesus".

Chapter Three
I Don't Want to
Be a Christian

epiphany - Pronunciation[i-pif-uh-nee] – noun, plural - nies.
   1. *a sudden, intuitive perception of or insight into the reality or essential meaning of something, usually initiated by some simple or commonplace occurrence or experience.*

You've all had a day like this; it's one of those rare "perfect" days. Things are just flowing into goodness. Everything that you see, hear, and feel, you place in your memory so you can reflect on it later. It may be one of those awesome moments in life when you have the great feeling of being connected with another person. I had one of those days recently. A young married couple had just arrived to be part of what God was doing here in our community and in our Tribe of Jesus. We sat under the shade of a tree on that warm day. It makes my heart happy to share with new friends in our Tribe what God has taught us about helping others understand the real and relevant Jesus, not the American Churchianity Jesus.

After that talk, I ran into another twenty-something friend who is in our Tribe. We talked about another friend and how he had grown closer to God in the past weeks. It was encouraging knowing our friend was seeking and finding the Spirit and reality of God in his life.

Before I drove home I decided to exercise and took a trail run along the floor of our mountain valley. The valley walls, thousands of feet above me, the clear river flowing next to me, the shades of pines and oaks, and the openness of meadows were all part of my run. As my trail traversed a meadow, my hands ran along the top of tall soft grass turned dry in the sun. I truly felt the goodness of God from the friends I had talked to that day and from the natural beauty that surrounded me.

In our area radio reception is almost non-existent. You can listen to three stations a great alternative rock station that comes in with a little bit of static, the country and western station that has a little bit clearer signal, and then with a powerful signal there's the Christian Talk station. I listen to this occasionally to stay somewhat informed about the mindset of Churchianity. About half of the time, the radio show content consists of sermons or Bible studies from churches, national and local.

So after this "perfect day", I was driving home and listening to this preacher. As he preached, there was a growing sense of irritation or some would describe as anger in his voice. At one point, yelling with an aggressive tone he shouts, "This country was founded on God's authority and we will NOT let it go!!" I immediately thought about how arrogant sounding and damaging his words would be to friends of mine who are searching spiritually. From the congregation listening to the preacher there was enthusiastic clapping and verbal affirmation of his statement. Then the preacher began making fun of atheists and agnostics. The crowd laughed in approval, followed by more of his angry words and shouting. I thought of my friends, former atheists and agnostics, who are now Followers of Christ. If they had heard this preacher and the laughter of the Christians, it might have driven them away from the love and life found in the person and teachings of Jesus.

While listening to this event on the radio I had an epiphany! It came to my mind in a clear and full sentence. From my heart and head, the following words entered my mind, "I don't want to be a Christian." The words had such clarity and reality to them that for a brief nanosecond it shocked me. But immediately the truth of it began to sink in. If this preacher and his church are representative of what a Christian is, I wanted nothing to do with it. Sadness was the overwhelming emotion I felt. I knew that probably most of the people in this church on the radio were probably part of my Christian family as children of faith in Jesus. It hurt my heart knowing they could be misled to think and act this way.

Once again, I yearned for a new term to identify myself spiritually. We call our group here the Tribe of Jesus, and we identify ourselves as Followers of Christ, Christ Followers. But even that term is lacking because I am never consistent in my journey as a Follower of Christ. There are days when Jesus and

I walk side by side; he teaches me, and I find great joy in His presence, like this "perfect day". There are other days when Jesus has trouble finding me. He calls out to me and I'm either distracted with stuff or due to selfishness I choose to ignore him.

If some of you reading this are Christ followers, you have been at this same place. You may be there right now. You understand that if you're walking with Jesus and you begin walking slightly away from his love and presence each day, it's not long before Jesus is just a distant blur in your spiritual vision. We understand how Christians or anyone can be misdirected to say and do things that are destructive and negative. Regardless of what Christians say and do, Jesus calls us to forgive and love them.

If you're not a Christ follower, we apologize for what we ourselves and other Christians have said or done out of selfishness, ignorance, sheer stupidity, egomania, or a quest for power. We can understand and forgive the negative actions of Christians, but that forgiveness doesn't translate into acceptance. If Jesus was walking around today, he could accuse many people and groups of false representation or unauthorized use of His name and message. Because someone claims to be a Christian or a group has "Jesus" in their name, it in no way means that Jesus is happy with their actions or that Jesus desires for them to represent His message and purpose.

Whenever the news media wants an evangelical or conservative Christian viewpoint on an issue they regularly go to a few national Christian leaders. At times when these men or women speak, my response is, "Thanks again for giving my friends another reason to dismiss Christianity and not have any desire to be associated with Jesus." It never helps when a Christian spokesperson makes a statement that a politician would be a worse potential office holder than if the Devil himself was elected. A pastor who describes someone as being worse than Satan for political reasons is not the way of Jesus. When Christian leaders make these statements on-air it would be great if Jesus walked into the television studio and we heard through the open microphone something like "Oh shit! It's Jesus!"

⌘ ⌘ ⌘

Jesus Story

Jesus and his buds (disciples) were hanging out at the lake. The pastors and church leaders had just demanded Jesus do a circus act miracle to prove to them that He was indeed from God. Now Jesus had already done some pretty cool stuff like making a blind guy have sight for the first time ever, healing a paralyzed man so he could walk and run home, and feeding thousands of people with basically just a family size bucket of fast food chicken.

Jesus told the pastors and church leaders "Are you serious? You pay attention to all sorts of other signs like looking at the color of the morning and evening sky to predict the weather and you have doubts about whether the miracles I did were from the power of God or not? Only a sick and twisted person would be asking me for another sign to prove God's power and presence within me! You should be just blown away and silly with happiness for the people whose bodies and lives were healed!"

Disgusted with the pastors and their supporters, Jesus turned to his followers and said, "We're out of here." They hopped a boat and sailed to the other side of the lake. After they landed and went ashore, they got hungry. One of the guys began asking, "Did anyone get any snacks or food back on the other side of the lake?" Then Peter probably chimed in, "No, I thought that was your job." They soon realized no one had brought any food.

Jesus, his mind elsewhere, then told them, "By the way, I'm warning you, don't take any of that junk food the pastors offer you." The disciples now hollered, "'Great! Now we'll really go hungry if we're limited about whom we can accept food from!" This was followed by a bunch of whining and complaining because there wasn't a grocery store anywhere around! On this day, Jesus had seen a lack of faith from those who should have had it, the pastors, and now he has to see a lack of faith from his best friends and companions.

Jesus irritated said, "You guys have such small faith! You have seen me feed thousands of people with a couple of granola bars and a turkey sub, and you're worried about having some bread now! Don't you understand I wasn't talking about real junk food earlier? So I'll say it again 'Beware of the junk food being offered to you by the pastors.'"

Now the group moved their thoughts from their stomachs being full to their spirits being full. From the events of the day and previous experiences, the disciples knew that the pastors offered an unfulfilling and misdirected understanding of God. They realized once again that Jesus offered and gave them the true life and message from God.

– Jesus Story from Matthew 16

⌘ ⌘ ⌘

Some pastors and Christians today are misdirected, have the wrong priorities, and offer others spiritual junk food. This may cause you to think, "I don't want to be a Christian" or "There's no way I'll become a Christian!" Right now, I encourage you to actually hang out with Jesus. Read his words and look at what he did. In doing this you will discover what his true message is, filtering out the noise and voices of the misdirected Christian spokespeople. I hope you'll clearly see the Jesus that is compassionate, transparent, honest, and loving. Jesus is a man, a teacher, a mentor and the God that you'll enjoy hanging out with. Don't slide or passively accept the easy path of the preferred spirituality of those around you. Think, study, question, and pray. Make an intelligent and informed decision to become a friend, student, and Follower of Jesus.

Do Something

First, realize that people who are Jesus Followers are not at all times the best representation of God's goodness. Christians have the same struggle as everyone else. Before you judge them, I challenge you to spend one day or a couple of days getting to know some Christians. Have you ever watched the reality show, "30 Days"? In the show, the producers choose a controversial or challenging social circumstance and place an individual in that situation for thirty days. The show records their personal experiences. Some of the shows included spending time in a county jail, trying to live on minimum wage, and having a Christian evangelical live with a Muslim family.

This is what I'm suggesting for you, but only for a day or two. There is bound to be a church or a student ministry that helps with an after school program for kids, the homeless or the elderly homebound. This will take some work on your part, but find out what's going on and volunteer to help out one day. As you interact with the Christians, focus and identify the positives in their lives. Email me and let me know what happens at steve@ohshititsjesus.com.

Please send your critical comments, encouragements, and questions to steve@ohshititsjesus.com. You can post your thoughts and join a discussion about the book and this chapter on www.ohshititsjesus.com and on the Facebook group "Oh Shit Its Jesus".

Chapter Four
There's Nothing
Holy About
This Book — The Bible

At our mountain community in the past, our Tribe has put on a drum circle in the woods during the dark summer nights. We would invite our friends to come sit around a campfire or lantern, play hand drums, and talk about spiritual and social issues.

At one drum circle, the topic of the Christian scriptures, the Holy Bible, came up. A couple of our friends expressed their beliefs about errors, contradictions, and biases within the Bible. They made their statements to dismiss the Bible as a flawed ancient writing and therefore not worthy to be given any serious consideration in a person's life.

I had a Bible with me so I took it from my pack, held it up and stated, "There is nothing holy about this book!" I then threw the Bible onto the ground in the middle of our circle. There was a shocked silence from some in the circle. Then I said, "The Bible is not holy, but the message is."

Let me try to explain this. You can respond to someone's objections to the Bible with historical facts and by comparing it to other ancient manuscripts and writings from other religions. This is important and gives objective support to the historical and contextual reliability of the Bible.

However, the trustworthiness of the Bible needs to be looked at from another perspective. First, why are most Americans repulsed or not interested in the Bible? What's your answer? Could it be that one major reason people reject the Bible is because some preachers and Christians use the Bible as a weapon to attack, hurt, and belittle people? When Christians are being buttheads and fighting whatever cultural enemy they have chosen to defeat, sometimes the first words out of their mouths are "The Bible says…" Good grief! Can we first have a conversation about someone's need or the reason for their beliefs?

At times when a Bible thumpers says "The Bible says…." , what they might be communicating is, The Bible says…

- to know God is to live a life of guilt
- pleasing God and being a true Christian means being a member of my church and subscribing only to my version of Christianity
- God hates homosexuals, abortion clinic workers, Liberals, Democrats, and any Christian who disagrees with my Biblical views. (*I have personally experienced this*)
- if you are faithful to God, then you will be wealthy and healthy (Meaning if you're not wealthy or healthy then somehow you've been unfaithful to God).

- you just need to accept God's truth, don't ever question it or try to actually intellectually evaluate it
- there is an answer for everything! There is no mystery of God. We as Biblical Christians understand and can explain all the spiritual and theological questions you can ask. Because, "the Bible says."

The Bible thumpers say that in the Bible, God has a long list of dos and don'ts, he expects you to obey if you really want to please Him;

DON'TS: no drinking alcohol, no smoking, no tattoos, no sinful music, no watching "R" rated movies, no hanging out with the ungodly, no belief in evolution, no woman pastors, etc. *(I'm sure you can think of a few more don'ts. When's the last time you've heard a preacher preach against the sin of gluttony or arrogance?)*

DO'S: Vote Republican, give ten percent of your money to the church no matter what your financial situation, be at every church meeting and event, talk to everyone you meet for the first time about Jesus or they're going to Hell, only be baptized the way our church does it to be true to God's Word, accept only the pastor's interpretation of the Scriptures, believe in a literal six day creation of the earth and universe, etc.

Most churches teach the "do's" of being loving, forgiving, and meeting each other's needs, but *some* churches simply ignore those teachings or interpret and apply them in negative way. We know what the Bible thumpers say, but what does the Bible itself say? It says a bunch of things that make sense. Many things that are amazing. Quite a few things that are confusing. But is it holy?

How do you personally define "holy"? That definition will determine whether or not you can ascribe that word to the Biblical scriptures of any other writings by man. For me, this is where I go with this. If something is holy, it is perfect, as God is perfect. Perfect meaning something is morally pure. To me "holy" is a word that can only be ascribed to an entity, not to a human. Holy is something beyond human; supernatural, something above our limited human abilities.

About forty people who were not morally pure wrote the Christian scriptures. Beware of any religious group whose beliefs are based upon the writings of a single person. The numerous Biblical writers completed their works over a period of about 2,000 years. Their writings together are a collection of memoirs, poetry, songs, historical narratives, spiritual visions, and personal letters. The early followers of Jesus wrote about their experiences with Jesus. They sent letters to encourage one another in their faith in the face of public opposition and deadly persecution. These writings became what are called the New Testament of the Christian scriptures. These early Followers of Christ did not think they were writing anything that was holy or that would ever be used as "Holy Scripture" by people in the future.

Then what were they writing? They were writing down the ancient oral stories that had been passed along through their Tribes for centuries. They wrote down the current events of their time and what God spoke and did at the time. They jotted down personal blogs about their experiences with the Spirit of God. They composed poems and songs about their difficult but joyous lives in following God. They penned very personal letters to their close friends. They compiled investigative accounts of this new belief in Jesus, and a few wrote intense and specific messages spoken to them supernaturally from God.

If you're a Christian reading this, answer this question, "What if all the copies of the Bible disappeared and the only way to communicate the message and life of Jesus was through our personal knowledge of what Jesus Christ said and did. Would our letters and writings about Jesus be considered "Holy scripture" by later generations of Christians?"

What is holy is how the Biblical writings have perfectly, miraculously, and supernaturally foretold about the life, person, and teachings of Jesus Christ over the centuries. That may sound like a load of crap to you, but it is honestly spooky how someone numerous centuries before Jesus was born would have known so many specific details about Jesus' birth, life, death, and resurrection. These details must have been revealed to them.

The only way to decide if this is valid is for you to check out the Biblical scriptural writings for yourself.

The Followers of Jesus believe Jesus is the actual embodiment of the spiritual God Creator to the physical Earth. We worship Jesus, God. We do not worship or "idolize" a book full of pages. Many in Churchianity worship the Bible instead of Jesus. There are a few times in the New Testament when the writers talk about the "Word of God". However, the New Testament writers weren't referring to the New Testament because it hadn't all been written or compiled yet. They were referring to the Hebrew Scriptures that they had at their point in history, our Old Testament.

One of the letters in the New Testament is from an unknown writer who was trying to encourage the faith of the early Followers to stay strong and continue in their beliefs and faith in Jesus. The Followers were suffering persecution for their beliefs. This is a quote from that writing. *"For the word of God is full of living power. It is sharper than the sharpest knife cutting deep into our innermost thoughts and desires. It exposes us for what we really are. Nothing in all creation can hide from him. Everything is naked and exposed before his eyes. This is the God to whom we must explain all that we have done."* (Hebrews 4:12-13, New Living Translation)

In the time of Jesus the term "Word of God" referred to a direct message from the Spirit of God or the message Jesus taught. One of the closest disciples of Jesus, John, along with other early Followers, refer to Jesus himself as the "Word" or the "Word of God" in their writings. This makes complete sense since the words Jesus spoke were the words of God. You'll notice in the passage above the pronoun changes from "it" to "him". If you replace those pronouns with "Jesus" it reads like this, "*For Jesus is full of living power. Jesus is sharper than the sharpest knife cutting deep into our innermost thoughts and desires. Jesus exposes us for what we really are. Nothing in all creation can hide from him. Everything is naked and exposed before his eyes. Jesus is the God to whom we must explain all that we have done.*" (Hebrews 4:12-13, Paraphrase)

Christians today will apply the term "Word of God" directly to the letters and writings of the New Testament. Instead, the term should be applied directly to Jesus and his message. It's crazy to have a relationship with a letter someone wrote. It makes no sense to worship the personal reflections and stories of an early Follower of Jesus as holy. Following Jesus and knowing God is about a real relationship. When Christians read the writings of the New Testament in a literal word for word interpretation and try to apply *some* of the cultural context from 2,000 years ago to our society and churches today, it is a recipe for misuse and misrepresentation of the message. Some relational and cultural truths are universal and apply to everyone over the ages. What's hurtful and destructive is when Christians interpret the scripture as they deem "the truth" and then consider anyone who disagrees with them to be a non-Christian, not saved, not Bible believing.

I love reading the Christian scriptures, the Bible. It has brought me so much joy, guidance, and personal meaning to know God as my "Spiritual Dad". It is humbling and great knowing God loves me and has adopted me into his family and the Kingdom of God. It is painful when I'm told by a Christian, that I personally don't believe in or respect the Bible, because our beliefs may be different.

Paul, the apostle and saint, was actually a "Christian Bounty Hunter" before he trusted Jesus with his life. He was ordered by the religious leaders to catch Christians so they could be thrown into prison or given the death penalty for their beliefs. Paul was traveling to hunt down more Christians when he had a personal experience with Jesus. He actually met Jesus as a live person after Jesus was executed by being put to death on a cross. This experience was life changing. As a Jewish religious scholar, his knowledge of the Judaic scriptures gave Paul the insight needed to believe that Jesus was indeed the promised Messiah. However, intellectual understanding alone is not how God desires to have a relationship with us. Paul's relationship with God changed when he allowed his heart and mind to accept the miracle and reality of who Jesus is.

A physician who wasn't raised as a Jew, Luke, became a Christ Follower and wrote about how Paul, called Saul at the time, became a Follower of Christ. You can find Luke's account about Paul's experience in what is called the Book of Acts in the ninth chapter.

Paul's courage and humility as a Christ Follower is a great model for Christ Followers. Paul and his writings are a powerful message from God to teach Christ Followers and help them trust Jesus in their everyday, walking around life. We must understand that Paul was a man like you and I. When Paul wrote his letters to Jesus' Followers, there is no way that he thought "I'm writing Holy Scripture that will be applied to a culture 2,000 years from now, where my every word will be argued over and affect the personal lives of millions of people." Therefore, when the New Testament writings are read, they need to be read understanding that the writers did not think they were writing Holy Scripture.

Some of what seemed correct to Paul in a foreign culture 20 centuries ago does not make sense and apply to our lives today. However, *much* of it does, because people and their nature as moral beings have not changed much over the past two millennia.

Within the writings of the New Testament we amazingly have historically and critically sound documents that over the centuries have provided us the message of Jesus and the experiences of the first Followers of Jesus. The Bible is not holy, but through the Spirit of God working in the lives of the New Testament writers we are told the message of a holy God.

Earlier I mentioned John, a disciple of Jesus. He was one of Jesus' closest friends during Jesus' three years of ministry. In the beginning of his book John uses the term "the Word" to identify Jesus. Following are the opening sentences of his book. I've replaced the term "Word of God" with "Jesus." Christians may disagree with each other over lots of theological crap, but following Jesus is what's important and that is why John mentions Jesus first! I hope that what John wrote speaks to your heart and mind.

⌘　⌘　⌘

Jesus Story

In the beginning, Jesus already existed. Jesus was with God, and Jesus was God. He existed in the beginning with God. God created everything through Jesus, and nothing was created except through him. Jesus gave life to everything that was created, and his life brought light to everyone. Jesus, the light, shines in the darkness, and the darkness can never extinguish his light. God sent a man, John the Baptist, to tell about the light so that everyone might believe because of his testimony. John himself was not the light; he was simply a witness to tell about the light, Jesus.

The one who is the true light, who gives light to everyone, was coming into the world. Jesus came into the very world he created, but the world didn't recognize him. Jesus came to his own people and even they rejected him. But to all who believed him and accepted him, he gave the right to become children of God. They are reborn—not with a physical birth resulting from human passion or plan, but a birth that comes from God. So Jesus became human and made his home among us. He was full of unfailing love and faithfulness. And we have seen his glory, the glory of the Father's one and only Son.

– Jesus Story paraphrased from John 1:1-14

⌘   ⌘   ⌘

Do Something

Discover Jesus, not answers. If you have never done it, read John's story about Jesus, written in the book of the Bible called John. If you have read it, read it again! If you've never read it, you can buy a Bible pretty much anywhere. I would suggest buying a modern translation. Understand that some parts will make sense, while other parts may be confusing. If you wrote an account of your life experiences, how confusing might it be for someone in the year 4008 to understand all the cultural and religious references in your writing?

The writings about Jesus, the Bible, were not meant to be an answer book in support of someone's scientific views or political agenda.

As you read John's experience, place yourself in the moment of the events, the emotions, the relationships and the physical surroundings. Discover the reality of Jesus' life and his message. Try not to get bogged down in philosophical and theological minutiae.

If you're a Christian, as you read John, forget everything that you've been taught. Don't read the scripture to simply validate what you've been taught. Actually read and listen to what is happening in the scripture. Some of your beliefs may be found, others may be nonexistent, and you may discover new truths and questions.

Please send your critical comments, encouragements, and questions to steve@ohshititsjesus.com. You can post your thoughts and join a discussion about the book and this chapter on www.ohshititsjesus.com and on the Facebook group "Oh Shit Its Jesus".

Chapter Five
What the Hell?

Have you ever had someone tell you to go to hell? Well, if you have, it probably wasn't a pleasant experience. But did the person actually mean they wanted you to spend a spiritual eternity in Hell? Probably not. Did the person who said that to you believe in an afterlife? Did they actually believe in a spiritual Hell, or were they just angry?

What would you think of someone who told you they honestly believed you would go to Hell and spend an eternity there? You'd be pretty upset and probably walk away, never to talk to that person again. You'd think, "Who do you think you are to determine my place in the afterlife?"

The roads in our mountain community are winding and dangerous. Trees, boulders, cliffs, and fast rivers border the roadways. As you can imagine, losing control of a vehicle is not a good thing to do. You can crash into the mountainside, career off the roadway into a steep river canyon or have a head on collision with another vehicle. The results can be serious, even deadly. One Halloween, a local employee was driving home after attending a Halloween party where he had been drinking alcohol. He crashed his car and died. Please don't drive under the influence or let a friend drive impaired. People care for you and love you. Don't endanger your life or the life or others.

For the sake of this story let's call the young man who died John. I know a friend of John's, let's call her Jane. She had recently moved away, but she heard the sad news of John's death. Emotionally shook up, Jane talked to her neighbor who was a "church going Christian" about her friend's death. Jane had planned to visit John during the Halloween holiday but changed her plans. Because of this, she felt guilty about John's death, believing that if she was there she could have possibly prevented the crash and his death.

The "church going Christian" neighbor asked if John was a Christian. Jane said she didn't think he was. Then the "church going Christian" said plainly and insensitively "Oh, then your friend is in Hell. If you're not a Christian then you go to Hell." You can imagine the pain and anger my grieving friend felt!

Seriously, what would cause you to say that to someone whose friend had just died?!! Or to anyone??!!! This "church going woman" reinforced many reasons why Jane was reluctant to accept Christianity. How Churchianity talks about Heaven and Hell causes many to feel hurt and have negative feelings about the church and Christ.

What are your beliefs about an afterlife? If you believe in a spiritual afterlife, what do you believe is the truth regarding the afterlife? Let's talk about *truth* and *belief* a little. Truth is not relative or subjective to a person's feelings or opinions. There cannot be billions of contrasting and contradictory realities of the afterlife originating from individual beliefs. In other words, you and I do not have the power to create and define spiritual reality and the afterlife based upon our personal views and opinions. Just because *you* believe something doesn't make it real or truthful.

Do you believe that you have the supernatural power to define and create the afterlife? Do you believe that you have the power to define and create God? How arrogant and prideful is it for us to think we have the power and authority to define God and determine the afterlife? If God is "God", if the afterlife exists, then God and the afterlife exist independent of our personal views and opinions.

Please think about and consider the following questions: "How and when has God related to mankind?" "Where has God's message been communicated?" "Who has understood and responsibly recorded and shared this message to others?" There are numerous groups that say they have the true message and answers. In searching, you will find that many of your friends believe they have the answers. As you listen to their answers you will find common themes, but you will also discover opposing and divergent beliefs.

You can choose to believe in one of the messages and answers you discover. But once again, your choice to believe does not determine reality and make it true. Believing in one of those messages, in something you cannot see is what is called "faith". Faith should not be a "blind faith", unwittingly accepting what others tell you to believe. Too many people's faith about God and the afterlife are based upon accepting teachings or beliefs they have never personally investigated.

What vision or images come to your mind when you think of Hell, a devil in a red suit, or fire and flames? Where do those visions come from? (*They do make for some great laughs in comedy skits and cartoons though.*)

Let's investigate our beliefs about the afterlife. What is Hell? Does Hell reside in the spiritual realm or is it a part of East Texas on a sweltering humid day in August? Could Hell be a place separated from the presence and goodness of God? Is Hell a place of pain and suffering?

If Hell is a place in the spiritual realm, a place separated from the goodness and presence of God and a place of pain and suffering, then wouldn't a loving God, who resides in the spiritual realm, do all He can to help everyone avoid such a place?

To help people avoid Hell, what images could God use? What picture of Hell could God paint so that no one would want to go there? The ancient view of Hell portrayed in the Bible is derived from a deep gorge in the southeast area of Jerusalem called the Valley of Hinnom. This valley was a place where certain religious groups would offer up child sacrifices to evil gods. After this practice ended, no one wanted to live in an area where innocent babies had been killed and evil gods had been worshiped. Therefore, the Valley of Hinnom became a garbage dump for the community. Hinnom was a location that would cause a feeling of revulsion within the community, a place of evil and death. Dead animals and even unwanted infants, would be killed and dumped in the Valley of Hinnom. This was a place you would not want to spend an eternity at.

What gas is produced from decaying stuff at a garbage dump? Methane! Methane catches on fire and can burn at the top of the dump or under the surface, hence, the image of a fiery Hell. Can you imagine the stench of burning animal hair, flesh, and garbage?!

Therefore, Hell has been associated with evil, death, the destructive power or fire, and the smell of decay and death. God gave us this vision and symbolic view of Hell so that it would cause a personal revulsion and reaction so strong we would do anything possible to avoid being in Hell.

We've investigated the image of Hell, but that still doesn't address the thought you may be having "A loving God would never send anyone to Hell." I totally agree with you, "A loving God would never send anyone to Hell." But you and I may be saying two different things. Let me explain. We discussed earlier what Hell is, "a place in the spiritual realm separated from the presence and goodness of God." So let's walk through this together.

What would cause a separation or a break between the people God created and God himself? What causes a break in the relationships you have with people? Someone may say or do something that angers and hurts you. They may treat you or others in an unfair or unkind way. They break the trust you have in them to be a faithful friend and to treat you in a kind way. If someone treats you with disrespect and breaks the trust you have in them, then the relationship is damaged or possibly over. However, you will probably try to restore the relationship later.

God is no different. God gave humans a sweet deal, the power of his presence evident in the beauty of the natural world, the spirit of his morality and love within our hearts, and his direct message of love, restoration, and peace through the ancient prophets and Jesus. What have people over the eons of time, done with all this goodness from God? Pretty much screwed it up, and spit in God's face! Wars, torture, exploitation of others, pursuit of selfish desires, indifference to others, lack of restraint, thoughts of revenge, hate, lies, and lack of concern for those around us is just a short list of how we have reacted to God's gift of life, free will, and spiritual existence.

Would you seriously want to hang out with someone who continually acted in a negative and horrible manner? Why invite someone to a party if they're going to be mean to you and your friends and be a total butthead? There are consequences for bad behavior in our relationships with people. There are consequences for our bad behavior in our relationship with God. However, God is a loving God and gives every person a second chance to be invited back to the "party." Some people seek out God's forgiveness and invitation back to the party. Others ignore God. Some tell Jesus to "F…Off!" and never accept God's desire to restore the broken relationship.

God loves you more than you can comprehend and desires a relationship with you. God wants you to experience his goodness and avoid the loss of not knowing him. God thought of the most miserable place he could think of, an abhorrent garbage dump, to hopefully help persuade you to seek him out and avoid the spiritual consequences of trying to be your own god. (So you know, I don't believe God has a specific gender. I'm using the male reference solely as a point of communication.)

I've had conversations with friends about God and they've made the comment that if God is powerful and cares so much about us, then why doesn't he just reveal himself and plainly tell us he exists? I've responded with, "I agree, and actually, he's already done that. That's who Jesus was." Jesus' followers believe that Jesus was God in the flesh. God came down as Jesus to die a horrible death to show to us how much he loves us. What would your thoughts be towards a friend who died in an attempt to restore a friendship with you or save you from a life-threatening situation? Sounds crazy, but think about that.

Jesus, being God, didn't have to die. However, Jesus allowed himself to be brutally tortured and executed to prove to us his love and his commitment to restoring our relationship with God. To prove that what he said was true and that he had the power and authority to say what he said about God and life, Jesus performed many supernatural miracles and came back to life after being dead for three days. That got a lot of people's attention! In fact, many of those who opposed Jesus and those who believed in him probably shouted, "Oh shit! It's Jesus!" when they saw him, but with opposing emotions, one of dread and the other of joy!

People who hear about Jesus and his miraculous life have the same reaction today. Some choose to acknowledge Jesus' amazing love and respond in kind. Others ignore and reject Jesus and his message. If that's you, you're missing out on a significant part of God's goodness. Do you want that to continue forever, for eternity? That would be Hell. Jesus invites you to come join the community of his followers. Come and hang out with the real Jesus, not the "agenda Jesus" of some churches, and you'll be surprised at what you'll see and hear.

That being said you might still be asking the question, "Why does anyone have to go to Hell?" You may also believe that Hell doesn't exist and that everyone goes to Heaven. At times when Jesus would be speaking to crowds or religious scholars, he would teach about Hell to make a point. So let's look at one of those.

⌘　⌘　⌘

Jesus Story

Jesus was hanging out in public and talking with friends and others who were interested in what he had to say. This included people the religious leaders in town wouldn't be caught dead with because it would soil their reputation. However, a few of the rich local religious leaders showed up just to ridicule Jesus. To make a point Jesus taught that if you let it, the desire and corruption of money will cause you to be dishonest, cheat others and push God out of your life. He taught that there is one thing that should direct your life, that's the love and wisdom of God. If you don't allow God to give you guidance in your life, then money or something else can have power over you and your life.

The religious leaders, who were loaded financially, heard this and mocked Jesus in front of his friends. Jesus, not taking any crap from these guys said, "For you guys it's all about image and you think that people respect you. However, God knows, and I know, that your hearts are evil. The 'titles' and the 'respect' that the people give you are because they think you speak for God. God, however, thinks you're full of it."

Then Jesus told them this story, "There was a rich guy who wore $5,000 suits, drove a $400,000 sports car, and lived in a mansion. Every day, at an intersection on this guy's drive to work stood a homeless guy, Larry, who was panhandling and holding a sign reading "God Bless You." Larry had diabetes and sores on his feet. Every day Larry hoped the rich guy in the sports car would at least give him some pocket change, but he never did. Sometimes, when Larry left the intersection at night, thieves would beat him up and steal his money."

"Well, Larry eventually died of the infections from the sores on his feet. The angels of God carried Larry's soul to Heaven. The dude with the sports car died soon afterward and his soul went to Hell. The rich guy looked toward Heaven and screamed out, "I'm burning alive in these flames! My parents went to church and my grandmother taught Sunday School, please have pity on me. Hey, I can see there in Heaven the homeless guy from the intersection. Please send him over here to just give me a drop of water to limit my agony a little!" One of the first followers of God, Abraham, a soul in Heaven responded, "In your lifetime you had everything that you wanted and lived in luxury. Larry, the homeless guy here, had nothing and lived in misery. So he is here now being comforted and now you are in torment. Besides this is Heaven and you are in Hell. There is a great spiritual separation between those that seek after God and those that ignore him. God does not allow anyone with him now in Heaven to leave and go to Hell where you are."

The rich guy then asked the soul in Heaven, "Okay, then can you at least send Larry to find my five brothers so he can warn them about Hell so they won't come here when they die?" But the soul from Heaven said, "Your brothers have already been warned. They've heard the message of God from relatives and other Followers of God. Plus they know about the writings of God's message and can read it at anytime."

Desperate, the rich man pleads, "But if someone like Larry who has died tells my brothers about Hell they will recognize their sins, seek out God, and follow him."

But the soul in Heaven says, "Your brothers did not listen to God's prophets from the past and they ignore the writings and message of God they have with them now. Therefore, they also won't listen to the message of God sent from someone who rises from the dead."

– Jesus Story paraphrased from Luke 16:1-31

⌘　⌘　⌘

Jesus performed miraculous healings, freed people from religious tyranny, and raised people from the dead. He was killed and came back to life. Jesus physically appeared alive after his public execution to hundreds of people and guess what? Individuals who saw this still didn't believe in Jesus' message or that he was the One sent to restore their relationship with God. What more does God have to do to get his message across?

There's plenty of Hell on earth among people. There's also quite a bit of Heaven on earth among people. It's painful and sad when the Hell on earth disturbs God's goodness on earth. It's comforting to know that in the spiritual world God separates good from evil; he separates that which is hellish from that which is heavenly. Who wants to spend an eternity with a drug dealer who still wants to deal, a child molester who's still looking for a victim, or a genocidal dictator still determined to continue his tyranny whatever the cost?

I still have a lot of unanswered questions about Heaven and Hell. I'm a human being, not God. Who goes to Heaven and who goes to Hell? I don't make that decision nor does any other mortal human! Ignore the simplistic and arrogant answers about Heaven and Hell given to you by some preachers and churches. Jesus welcomed into Heaven with him people who once were convicted criminals, unethical tax collectors, prostitutes, and prideful religious leaders. They had their lives changed by believing in and following Jesus. In the stories of Jesus, we hear about oppressed women, fishermen, soldiers, wealthy merchants, children, and politicians that placed their spiritual hopes in Jesus. Through Jesus' love, forgiveness, and restoration they had their lives changed for eternity.

Who do you welcome into your home? People you know, those you have a relationship with. Strangers are even welcomed into your home if they have relationships or are associated with others you trust. People are welcomed into your home not based upon a trust survey or a test they take. You welcome others into your home based on relationships, not based on a determination of just how good or bad someone has been. I believe Heaven and God are the same.

Who are the people not welcomed in your home? People you don't know or those who have broken the trust you've extended to them. God loves everybody and desires that everyone be in a loving and eternal relationship with him. God extends an invitation to us for a relationship with him by knowing Jesus. Here on earth, and in the spiritual realm, if we ignore Jesus, reject the goodness of God, and pursue our own selfish desires, there will consequences in our lives. I've seen it in my own life. You can see the results every day in the chaos and hardships across the world. God doesn't send someone to Hell. People make decisions to pursue a path away from God and his message, and they choose to separate themselves from God now and for eternity.

To give somewhat of a summary, here's where I stand on this whole issue of Heaven and Hell. A loving God will clearly separate and make a judgment call on good and evil. It's unloving if evil is not held accountable. It would be unfair and unjust if evil was not dealt with. A loving God does not force anything on anybody. God is not going to force someone into an eternal relationship with him in Heaven if they had rejected God's invitation to know him.

Having to reach some level of good karma or perform some religious rite to be included in Heaven is unjust and unloving. If someone is accepted in Heaven based upon one's efforts to achieve a certain level of morality or enlightenment; that leads to spiritual corruption and manipulation here on earth. That is not a loving God.

I believe if you're a nomadic herdsman in Mongolia who has never had a chance to hear the stories and message of Jesus, God will not automatically send you to Hell due to a spiritual law that God himself is forced to abide by. That never was Jesus' message.

In Heaven, I believe there will be nomadic herdsmen from Mongolia, but some pastors of churches in America will not be there. I say all of this to make the point that I don't know who goes to Heaven and who goes to Hell. Once again, that's not my call. I do know what Jesus taught us to do. Jesus told us to love others, tell others his message of love and forgiveness, and help them connect with God and follow him.

Hell is real. Everyone should search and make choices to avoid the hell of not knowing God and being separated from him for eternity. I hope and pray that you and I can pause, take a deep breath, and start the adventure of hearing the real message of Jesus. Our focus should be on knowing Jesus and having his spirit in our lives. I hope we'll see and experience the real impact a relationship with Jesus can have in our lives and in the world around us!

Do Something

Ask yourself what are the real life, spiritual benefits you might miss by not considering the message and person of Jesus. If God exists, if Jesus is the real deal, what could a spiritual relationship with Jesus bring to your life now and in the afterlife? Consider it, dwell on it, pray on it, see what happens. Let me know how that works for you.

Please send your critical comments, encouragements, and questions to steve@ ohshititsjesus.com. You can post your thoughts and join a discussion about the book and this chapter on www.ohshititsjesus.com and on the Facebook group "Oh Shit Its Jesus".

Chapter Six
Dark Matter, Dinosaurs, Darwin, & Dark Chocolate

All right, would you agree to the following – one of the main reasons you think Christianity is "full of it" is because the church ignores scientific fact and reason, particularly concerning the origins of the universe, the earth, and homo sapiens? Well, am I correct? You believe there's no way that the Milky Way, our solar system, and the earth were created in six days or even 6,000 years! You probably also believe it's ludicrous to think that man was formed out of the dirt of the earth and that two individual people, Adam & Eve, are the "parents" of the entire human race.

I agree with you. I'm a theoevolutionist and a follower of Jesus Christ. I have a Master's degree and I believe the message in the Bible is true. You may be thinking, "What? You can't be a Christian that accepts the Bible as truth and also believe in evolution. Plus, Christians are supposed to be misguided, ignorant, inbred, fanatics. (Okay, maybe the inbred statement is a little too much.)

There are millions of Christians with bachelor's and master's degrees in science, from state universities, who believe in and follow Jesus Christ as the Son of God. There are even Nobel Prize winners who are Christians, Charles Townes in Physics, Frank Wilczek in Physics, and former President

Jimmy Carter was awarded the Nobel Peace Prize. President Carter has a science degree and served in the Navy nuclear submarine program. The people listed previously are just a very small example of very intelligent individuals, doctors, and scientists who are Followers of Christ.

Scenario – You're stopped on the freeway or at a stoplight. The car in front of you has bumper stickers and window decals. Judging by the stickers, and even the type of vehicle (*old hippie van or new sports utility vehicle*), you believe that you can easily determine the political affiliation and religious beliefs of the driver in front of you. Am I right?

Here are the stickers you would see on my small politically correct foreign made crossover vehicle – an American flag with the word "Think" where the stars should be, a Yosemite park sticker, my wilderness first responder sticker, a NASA decal, and a Houston Texans sticker. Do you have any thoughts yet on "who I am"? Here are two others I failed to mention. I have a Christian "fish" sticker. Next to it, I have a silver decal of a dinosaur eating a Christian "fish" symbol. Besides making me laugh, the sticker and decal are there for a reason. I'm hoping that the two "opposing" stickers will make people think a little outside their culturally formed biases concerning evolution and Jesus.

Every now and then I have the joy of performing a wedding ceremony for a local couple. Such was the case one spring. The bride was from Nevada, so the wedding was there. The groom was from

California. His best man, the best man's wife and another friend traveled to Nevada together. At the rehearsal dinner, they parked behind my car on the side of the street. They saw the decals on the back of my car and began to wonder what they meant. A couple of hours before the wedding the best man came up to me and said, "I have a question for you. We saw the decals on your car last night, the Christian fish symbol, but then also the dinosaur eating the fish. We were wondering 'What does that mean? Could it be that some Christians have different views concerning evolution?' We asked (the groom & bride) about it and they said, 'You need to ask Steve. That's one of the reasons he's the Pastor doing our wedding.'"

I then had a great chance to explain that yes, there are Christians who are theoevolutionists. In the BIG PICTURE, concerning our relationship with God, understanding how the world and universe were created does not determine God's acceptance and love for us. Please don't think I'm discounting the scientific process. I love scientific exploration and study. However, regarding our spiritual lives, the focus should be on knowing the God who is the force behind the principle of causality enabling everything, and I mean everything to exist.

I told the best man that it is a shame that all the time and energy that Christians exert on battling evolution isn't used to help their neighbors and to meet the needs of the community. Using the opportunity, I shared with him a short Jesus story about a time when Jesus was asked by religious leaders, "What is the greatest commandment?" This question, to reword it, is asking Jesus, "What is the most important thing that God desires for us as people to focus on?" Jesus answered that what God wants us to do is to love God as much as we can, with our whole being, and then love and care for those around us as much as we care for ourselves and our own families. If we do that, then the world will truly be changed for good.

The best man nodded and agreed that we should focus on the big picture of helping others and seeking out God. It felt like this was his first exposure to a Christian that didn't fit into the stereotype that he, his wife, and their friend possibly had. I hope that hearing the truth that what God desires is a loving relationship with us and not agreement on a scientific principle is a small step for them in knowing the real Jesus.

When I was a young kid I remember looking up at the sea of stars in the night sky and thinking, "Wow, there must be a God." I began attending church soon after that. However, my stargazing did not end. I purchased a small telescope and was enthralled by the shadows cast within lunar craters and felt inspiration when viewing the reality of the rings of Saturn. If you haven't looked at the moon or the planets through a telescope you need to! It's so exciting seeing these heavenly lights as real objects and places! Viewed through a telescope it feels like you can almost reach out and touch the lunar surface. It's quite a different experience than seeing a photo in a textbook or online.

Naturally, I became seriously interested in space exploration and astronomy. As a teenager, I was a member of the press corps at the NASA Manned Spacecraft Center in Houston. I was a technical advisor providing information and analysis of the Apollo 17 lunar landing and the Skylab space station for a radio station covering the missions.

In college, I started backpacking and studied as much natural and environmental science as I could. From that time on I have never had a time when science seemed to conflict with my faith in Jesus. As a matter of fact, when I read about evolutionary adaptations, orogenesis (mountain building), dark matter, dark energy, or exobiology my belief and faith in God is made stronger, not challenged. Learning about the fantastic complexities and the powerful forces that enable life to exist on Earth or anywhere else is truly amazing. Our evolution and development as an intelligent species has always been a tenuous one. We have been one asteroid, one pandemic, or one variant in solar activity away from existing as a species. I believe our existence is the working of a divine Creator and not a random occurrence of cosmological events.

Here's a quote for you to think about by James Tour Ph.D., Organic Chemistry, Professor at Rice University, Department of Chemistry and Center for Nanoscale Science. "I stand in awe of God because of what he has done through his creation. Only a rookie who knows nothing about science would say that science takes away from faith. If you really study science, it will bring you closer to God." Quote from The Case for Faith, Lee Strobel, Zondervan, 2000; p.156.

We exist, and the universe is incredible! I don't care if it happened through God using billions of years of evolutionary process or through God using some kind of supernatural silly putty! I just love the fact that God cared enough to create us and the wonder of everything else in the universe.

Christians and the church waste a gigantic amount of time and energy talking about dinosaurs and humans coexisting, cataclysmic floods, and "genetic purity"(to explain Adam & Eve living for centuries) to defend their views of Biblical interpretation. On the positive side, some churches spend a huge amount of money and effort on serving those in need and addressing social justice. However, I often wonder how much greater the positive impact of the church and individual Christians could be if all the time and energy spent by Christians to prove "creationism" and "intelligent design" were directed towards the needs of their neighbors and friends.

As I've said many times, I believe that the Bible, the writings of the prophets, and the stories of the ancient ones were never meant to be regarded as or interpreted as a science book. I believe it's actually demeaning to view the scriptural writings as such. Believing in Jesus as the one true messenger of

God, the Messiah, and having a relationship with God through faith in Jesus has nothing, and I mean nothing, to do with a "six day creation", Darwin, or dinosaurs. Being able to know and have a relationship with a God that can create something from nothing, now that's huge! Think about this sequence of events – absolutely nothing, then Big Bang, coalesced molecules, gravitational forces, gaseous clouds, stellar formation, proto-planetary discs, planetary systems form, add some divine intervention, and now you can sit under the shade of a tree and enjoy a dark chocolate candy bar with a friend. You enjoying dark chocolate with a friend is more important to God than you accepting a "correct" view of creationism.

Because of my beliefs on this issue, I've had Christians doubt my relationship with God and tell me that I must not believe in the Bible. It's troubling and heart breaking to know that many people over the years have avoided having a spiritual conversation with me and other followers of Christ because of this nonexistent "barrier" between the Bible and science.

Here's what I would like to see happen. You, as a spiritual seeker or skeptic can sit down with a "Bible believing" Christian and actually have a friendly discussion. If you know a Jesus person, buy them some dark chocolate and sit down for conversation. *(There's some great biochemistry involved in eating a dark chocolate candy bar.)* Talk about your lives, struggles and joys, friends and families. You will find that you have much in common with each other. Pretty soon dinosaurs and Darwin won't seem that important.

What's my point in all of this? Focus on what is really important and true. By "really" I mean not what you and I decide is true, but what is the reality of the world. At the end of the day, what's most important to every person on earth? Could it be peace, family, friends, survival, or is the most important thing "doctrinal purity" on the issue of creationism?

At the end of our physical lives what's most important? Is it an ideological belief regarding how the universe was formed or the reality of having a relationship with the God who made you and loved you? This path towards love and life can be found in the way of Jesus. You can discover Jesus without all the crap about evolution and creationism mucking everything up. When you pursue and discover the truth about what Jesus taught and how he lived, it will hopefully change your negative reaction of "Oh shit! It's Jesus!" to one of positive anticipation and experience. The following Jesus Story helps us focus on the really important and impactful question we should be asking ourselves.

⌘   ⌘   ⌘

Jesus Story
Jesus was teaching in the towns around the Sea of Galilee, a large inland fresh water lake – think Lake

Tahoe. He decided to head back to Capernaum, his current hometown on the north shore of the lake.

It was known throughout the area, and especially in Capernaum that Jesus had cured some people from diseases and actually healed a Roman officer's servant who couldn't walk. Word spread through town that Jesus was back. Somewhere in the city was a man who had been paralyzed, a paraplegic, who could no longer work and could only beg and exist on the charity of others. Let's call this guy Ryan. Ryan's friends and family members when they heard Jesus was back, rushed from the fields and shops to go get Ryan.

Lying on his mat, Ryan's despair and hopelessness had migrated to a life of accommodation, but a prevailing sense of loss dwelt within him. Then his friends came and grabbed the sides of his mat. They were shouting over each other that Jesus was back in town and something about taking him to be healed. They lifted Ryan up and began hurrying down the hard packed dirt road.

Jesus walked from the lakeside dock through the city. A small crowd began to grow with each passing street. Interspersed within the men, women, and kids encircling Jesus were the local religious leaders. It was their belief that if someone was injured or ill in a serious way, like Ryan, it was God's way of punishing someone because of some sin they had committed. This is an outrageous and destructive cultural belief that unfortunately exists in various forms today.

Rushing around one corner, the friends carrying Ryan ran into Jesus and this moving group of people. With hope and faith the friends lowered Ryan to the ground in front of Jesus. Seeing Ryan's anxious hope and the faith of his friends, Jesus tells Ryan, "Take heart, son! Your sins are forgiven."

Immediately, some of the religious leaders turned their heads towards each other and said in a somewhat hushed tone, "This is blasphemy! Who does Jesus think he is? Does he think he's God?" Jesus, using his God "super-powers" knew what they were saying and thinking. He directly confronted them by asking, "Why are you so evil? Are you so self-absorbed and arrogant that you don't care for this man's spiritual well being? Since you're such experts on spiritual matters, here's a question for you. Which is easier to say to this man, 'Your sins are forgiven' or 'Get up and walk'? I will prove that I am God in the flesh, the Messiah, and have the power and authority to forgive sins." Jesus turned and looked down at Ryan. He tells Ryan "Stand up, pick up your mat, and go on home, because you are healed!"

In a truly mind blowing scene, Ryan actually leaps to his feet! Standing, he leans over picks up his mat and walks home. For many watching, they felt a sense of fear being in proximity to Jesus, someone with a supernatural power over life and body. Many began shouting praises to God for seeing an unbelievable miracle occur right before their own eyes. To the consternation and revulsion of the pastors and the pious, the Almighty God was actually standing before *them as a regular person, not as a burning bush or glowing white figure. God in human form was a field laborer with dirty feet who had the power and authority to forgive sin and to make a paralyzed man walk.*

– Jesus Story paraphrased from Matthew 9:1-8.

⌘ ⌘ ⌘

During this event the religious leaders' opposition to Jesus was based upon their culturally derived belief that Jesus did not and could not have the power to forgive this man's sin and repair his relationship with God. They were more concerned about their religious agenda than Ryan's spiritual well-being. Jesus knew Ryan, being paralyzed, had a great physical need. Jesus knew a greater need in Ryan's life was to be restored in a relationship with God. Jesus focused on that and forgave his sins. Ryan had been burdened with a socially imposed feeling of guilt and shame. Jesus came and removed that burden and lie from him.

As Ryan's life went on, we can surmise that he eventually found new work and adjusted to a walking around life. He would praise God and thank Jesus throughout his days for the new life given to him. People would see him years later and say, "There's goes Ryan. Did you know that he used to be paralyzed? Jesus, the Messiah, spoke and healed him with the power of God!" Kids would come to

Ryan and say, "Ryan, tell us the story again about how Jesus healed you!"

It seemed silly and ludicrous now as Ryan told the story, that the religious leaders and others doubted Jesus had the power and authority of God. Why? Because everyone in the village knew someone who had seen Jesus that day when Ryan had a miracle come into his life. There were people in town that had talked with witnesses who with their own eyes had seen Jesus rise from the dead after being brutally crucified and placed in a tomb for three days. Jesus had the power over his own physical death. Think about that. Who could have that kind of power? Who would have the power to make someone walk who is paralyzed?

Days, months and years from now what will you think about Jesus? Will you allow a meaningless religious argument over creation and evolution to cause you to miss out on a relationship with Jesus? Your friends may be shouting at you, "Blasphemy! How dare you even consider Jesus as God in the flesh?" At times, our spiritual lives are "paralyzed" by the cultural and religious crap that surrounds us. Jesus desires to free you from spiritual paralysis so that you can walk towards what's really important. What's important to God? God desires for you to know him and have a relationship with him through his life as Jesus, a guy with dirty feet from the hills and lakeshores of ancient Israel.

Do Something

Next time you see a Christian fish decal on a car or hear someone using the Bible as a science book, look at the trees; be in awe of clouds and the hues of sunlight splayed against them! Be amazed that the God who has the power to make the wonder of nature loves you and desires to know you. Focus on that.

Please send your critical comments, encouragements, and questions to steve@ohshititsjesus.com. You can post your thoughts and join a discussion about the book and this chapter on www.ohshititsjesus.com and on the Facebook group "Oh Shit Its Jesus".

Chapter Seven
The Church Sucks

So the church sucks? Is this the church that you attend now? Or maybe the Christian churches you've gone to a couple of times? Or could it be that you've never actually attended a church, but it's your opinion that the church sucks?

Whatever the case, you're absolutely right; there are indeed *some* churches that suck. To have this discussion, you and I have to define what we mean by "suck". Wikipedia defines "sucks" as a "term of general disparagement, indicating the subject or situation has no redeeming qualities" or "indicating a particular area of deficiency."

Take the first definition, "no redeeming qualities", that's a pretty harsh pronouncement on a group of people. I'm trying to think of some social or religious affiliated groups that I would proclaim as having "no redeeming qualities"? The KKK for sure, Al Qaeda and Osama bin Laden definitely. International Islamofascist terrorists who are responsible for thousands of innocent people's deaths and the beheading of those they have kidnapped, have no redeeming qualities.

What does "redeeming" mean? One definition of redeem is "to change for the better". Do we then mean by "sucks", that the church does not have any qualities that help an individual or a community "to change for the better?" A personal negative experience with a specific church can definitely cause you to believe that the church does not have a redeeming quality of seeking a change for the better in someone or in a community.

A small number of churches do express views that are destructive to the well being of our communities. The churches that are destructive tend to show up in media reports and television news shows. However, the majority of churches are feeding the homeless, conducting after school tutoring for kids, providing counseling for troubled marriages, and preparing meals for those who are ill and housebound. Some churches do indeed "suck;" but the vast majority of churches and the people in them are caring and loving, having many redeeming qualities and seeking to make many changes for the betterment of their community and their world.

This leads us to the second definition of "sucks", having a "particular area of deficiency." Let's think this through. The church is made of people, like you and I, human beings.

Answer this question. In your relationships and interactions with people, have you ever had a moment when you "sucked"? Have you ever been deficient in treating someone in a kind and caring manner? If you and I are honest, the answer, of course is yes; we have sucked at times in our relationships with people. I'm not presenting an excuse here. I still believe like you, that some churches do indeed suck.

What I am presenting is a dose of reality. No one is a perfect person. Groups consist of imperfect people. Any large group is going to have individuals that 'suck,' who have moments of deficiency, and are, at that time, a negative representative of that group. This, of course, is also true within churches, civic, environmental, political, and any other social group.

As Christ Followers, we seek out the love and guidance of God to help us make judgments and choices in life that are positive for ourselves and the community. I know that I have said or done things to cause someone to think the church sucks. When confronted by friends about these negative actions, we should appreciate the caring attitude of our friends and strive to correct the wrongs we have done. The poor choices and a lack of responsibility by some Christians and church leaders have caused people to make the following statements: "The church sucks!" "Why would I want to be a Christian, it'll just make me a worse person?" "Why should I consider Christianity as an option for my spiritual life? The Christians I know live just like me and I'm happy now without Jesus."

Answer the following questions. Are there schools that are poor schools? Are there some restaurants that you'll never eat at again? Are there leaders of charitable groups that use contributions to drive around in a high-end luxury cars? Yes, there are schools, restaurants, and charity groups that suck big time! But that doesn't mean you stop supporting education, never eat out again, or never give to a needy cause.

Concerning eating out, there's that one restaurant that has the perfect atmosphere and perfect tacos that you can't stop going to and talking about. The outside of the restaurant may need painting or the seating may be uncomfortable, but you still go because of the quality of what they offer and the social environment. There are churches out there that are serving up awesome portions of Jesus' love. I encourage you to keep searching for a church that, even though it's filled with people who like you and I, can suck from time to time, has the redeeming quality of changing things for the better and offers up a rewarding and "tasty" message of Jesus' love.

I say this in another chapter, but if you know of a church or a Christian who sucks in someway, let them know about it. Talk with them in a friendly and respectful way, but you need to let them know. Hopefully, your care and honesty will break through their Churchianity veneer so they'll understand and be willing to make changes.

⌘　⌘　⌘

Jesus Story

Once again, the religious leaders of Jesus' day were trying to come up with a question to ask Jesus in public, hoping that his response would thwart his growing popularity and following. These religious leaders had defined over six hundred laws regarding personal life and spiritual behaviors. They often debated about which ones were more important than the others. Because honestly, how realistic is it to follow over six hundred rules correctly so that God will love you? The message of Jesus was not about "do's and don'ts" but about a life changing relationship with the God of the universe.

The leaders were hoping that Jesus would pick or omit a certain law that they could argue with him about. They hoped that his followers might doubt his authority as a spiritual leader and teacher. A leader asked, "Teacher, which is the most important commandment in the Law of Moses?" This religious expert in the law was thinking to himself, "Man I got this! I'll be all over whatever this poor, uneducated day-laborer says."

Jesus responds "Easy. First and most important you must love the Lord your God with all your heart, all your soul, and all your mind. Then intertwined with that commandment, you must love and care for your neighbor just as much as you love and care for yourself and your family. If you do this, then all the other commandments will find meaning in your life. These two things - loving God and loving others - sum up all the words that God has shared through the ancient prophets and messengers."

– Jesus story paraphrased based on Matthew 22:34-40.

⌘   ⌘   ⌘

So yes, the church sucks at times because it's full of flawed people, just like you and I. But that should not be our focus. Our focus should be on knowing God and serving others in a community. The early followers of Jesus, many who centuries later have been given the title of Saints by the church, were really just normal people like you and I. These first followers decided to actually follow what Jesus said and many of them were killed because of it. They loved God with everything they had and with their whole being. In their homes they gathered together to talk about the new life and hope they had found in believing in and following Jesus. They loved the unlovable and showed Godly kindness and forgiveness to those who hated them and killed their loved ones. They helped to guide those who hated them towards a redeeming life, the life that seeks to know God and to make the world a better place. Christ Followers are living out this God given love in places like Communist China and a few Muslim countries where Christians are imprisoned and killed because of their faith in Jesus.

This love, from Jesus, transformed the world. Some churches today still contain this "Jesus love" and help to transform their communities for good. This courageous and powerful love also helps restore and free individual lives from the self-centered focus that entraps them. This new life from the love of Jesus thrills God and makes Jesus' death worth it. A few Christians and churches do not share the authentic love of Jesus. This makes God sad and causes Jesus to weep.

Do Something

This is the reality handed to us. No church is perfect because no one person is perfect. If we stopped associating with our friends and family who are not perfect, just as we are imperfect, we would have a very lonely existence. What can you do about a sucky world and churches that suck? Try loving God and loving those around you. Every day and in every situation, in every thought and action you have, you have a choice to love someone or perform an act of kindness to someone. Don't expect anything in return. Simply receive the joy of knowing you have tried to make someone's day better or happier. May God give you strength and wisdom in that and please let me know how that works for you.

Please send your critical comments, encouragements, and questions to steve@ ohshititsjesus.com. You can post your thoughts and join a discussion about the book and this chapter on www.ohshititsjesus.com and on the Facebook group "Oh Shit Its Jesus".

Chapter Eight
Jesus, Liberator of Women & Social Revolutionary

What do you think about Christianity when it comes to the subject of women's rights? Of course, your answer will depend on your personal experiences and the information that has been available to you.

One summer I met a friend of a friend who became a friend. This friend, a young woman, had left the church and her identity as a Christian. One of the main reasons that she pushed away from the church was the church's treatment of women. Unfortunately, her experiences of how "the church" relates to women, were derived almost solely from the experiences growing up in her hometown.

Let's see if what my friend experienced regarding women and the church is similar to what you've heard or been taught. She was taught that men are the only ones who can hold the title of Pastor, Priest, Deacon or any decision making role in the church; in a church, women should only teach lessons to children or other women. All decisions in a marriage and family are subject to the authority of the husband; wives should "submit" to their husbands as their spiritual leaders and as the head of the household; therefore, the husband has the final say on all decisions.

This is a patriarchal view of culture and relationships where, "Men lead and women follow." Jesus taught and lived out quite a different perspective on women's roles. However, once again the reality of Jesus' teaching has once again been distorted by the culture. Jesus in his life and teachings gave respect and honor to women. Women filled crucial and important roles in his purpose of showing God's love and telling God's message.

What would happen if Jesus came back from Heaven and spoke at a conservative church about the role of women in the church? Jesus would walk up to the pulpit, having to introduce himself because no one would recognize him from all the portraits of him in church. (Jesus is actually a dark skinned middle-eastern male with a beard, not an Anglo-Saxon with blond hair.) Jesus would begin talking about the equality of women in roles such as pastors, deacons, elders, teachers, etc. Unfortunately, the preachers and many people in the church would be thinking,"What is Jesus talking about? Doesn't Jesus know the Bible says…?"

⌘　⌘　⌘

Jesus Story
Jesus and his disciples, the followers wanting to learn about and apply the message of Jesus to their lives, were traveling to Jerusalem on foot. Along the

way, they stopped in the village of Bethany. Jesus' message and his popularity among the people had spread through all the villages in the area. A woman who lived in Bethany, Martha, invited Jesus and his friends to her house for a meal.

At this time in Jewish culture, women were not allowed to receive a religious education in the synagogue, the local Jewish churches. Only adolescent boys and men were allowed to receive an education at the synagogue. When women attended a religious service, they were not allowed to even sit with the men. They had to sit in the back, separated from the men by a wall. It would be considered a sin and culturally unacceptable to have men and women together in the same place being taught by a Rabbi.

The following is a quote from Rabbi Eliezer, a Jewish teacher of the first century, "Rather should the words of the Torah be burned than entrusted to a woman…Whoever teaches his daughter the Torah is like one who teaches her obscenity."

This was the cultural conception of women when Jesus and his disciples came to Martha and Mary's house for that meal. Others in the village heard that Jesus was at Martha's, and they rushed over to come and hear what Jesus would say and teach. Jesus used this as an opportunity to teach the people who had gathered around about the Kingdom of God. In a respectable Jewish home, where should the women of the house be when a meal is being prepared? In the kitchen, of course, helping to cook and prepare the meal. Mary, however, had the audacity to actually sit among the men and be taught by the Rabbi Jesus!! Mary wasn't sitting at the back of the room sneaking in on the meeting. No, she was sitting right up front at the feet of Jesus! This is a Rosa Parks, "Go to the back of the bus" moment! (If the American public school system has failed you and you don't understand that reference, do a search on the internet.)

Martha is shocked! She is busily performing her duties by preparing the meal while her sister Mary is sitting among the men and not helping her. Not wanting to "teach" the teacher about the social inappropriateness of what Mary was doing, Martha however finds a moment and tells Jesus, "Lord, doesn't it seem unfair to you that my sister just sits here while I do all the work? Tell her to come and help me."

Jesus, looking at her eye to eye, kindly says, "Martha you have a great heart. You care so much for the needs of others. But you're getting all worked up about some man-made rule and the busyness of doing what's expected. In the big picture, what's the most important thing right now? There is only one thing that anyone should get all worked up about – seeking God, soaking up as much of his love and truth as you can, and then helping others have God's love and peace in their everyday lives. This is exactly what Mary is seeking and has discovered. So for right now let's allow her to stay here and experience what God has to say to her."

– Jesus Story paraphrased from Luke 10:38-42.

⌘ ⌘ ⌘

In some Christian churches the "walls", the barriers, to women "sitting at Jesus' feet" and serving as pastors and leaders have been removed. Jesus was way ahead of our culture's "enlightened" perspective on the issue of women's spiritual equality.

When Jesus entered a town, swarms of people would come to hear him teach. Some would come seeking to be cured from an illness or injury. To keep from causing an unmanageable crowd in the villages, Jesus would use outdoor settings to be with the people, like a hillside or the shore of a lake. The outdoor settings were in complete contrast to the institutional buildings that the religious leaders of the day taught in. On a hillside, Jesus taught in a setting where there were no separate rooms or walls separating men from women in the church. Sitting on the cool grass of a hill, boys and girls heard that they were not insignificant, and that God loved them equally. The people who gathered at a lakeshore to hear Jesus teach were a beautiful mix of men and women, the young and old, babies and children. Therefore, when Mary sat down at Jesus' feet in a room full of men to listen to and be taught by God, it was something that the early followers of Jesus grew to experience, understand, and accept.

Many pastors and Christians on the "inside" of today's church need to spend more time outside the walls of the church, where the people of their community live and gather in the real world. Jesus would tell them, "Become a better Christian by stop going to church so much!" Church people need to experience the reality that everyone in their community is loved by God no matter what their gender, economic status, political preference, ethnicity, sexual orientation, etc.

Even in the early part of Jesus' teaching there was intense opposition to his revolutionary message. After spending some time in Jerusalem, Jesus decided to travel north back to Galilee. Jesus knew he had many more people to teach and more of the afflicted to heal before his deadly confrontation in a few years with the established religious leaders.

The shortest and most direct route back to Galilee was to travel north through a region called Samaria. However, any good religious person from Jerusalem would avoid traveling through Samaria by taking a loop around the area. The religious people took this annoying and hard detour because the saw the Samaritans as spiritual half-breeds. Centuries earlier these people had intermarried with non-Jews, which was seen as a betrayal to God. They established their own Temple and priesthood separate from the other Jews in and around Jerusalem.

To travel through Samaria would violate a huge cultural taboo and cause any religious person to be seen as "impure." By being at a place and with people that were considered to be sinners or unrighteous would tarnish one's reputation among other religious people. As Jesus walked and took the trail heading to Samaria the disciples may have thought "Samaria – really?! Are you serious?"

⌘   ⌘   ⌘

Jesus Story

Jesus and his buds were walking through Samaria in the warm late spring sun. It's about noon when they arrive at the Samaritan village of Sychar. As they approach the ancient well of Jacob, the disciples decide to go into town to fetch some food. A woman coming out to the well walks past the disciples as they headed into the village. Jesus stayed at the well and soon the woman showed up to draw her water for the day. Thirsty and tired from the journey, Jesus asked the woman for a drink of her water from the well.

The woman, let's call her Samantha, is shocked that Jesus spoke to her! A Jew, especially a man, should not be talking with a Samaritan or a woman in public. She tells Jesus, "I'm sorry, but I'm a Samaritan woman so why the heck are you talking to me? And you expect me to give you a drink?"

Samantha had an attitude, a chip on her shoulder. Why? Her life sucked. All the people in town thought of her as the town tramp or slut. She had shacked up with five men in town who had no respect for her, using her for their sexual and emotional needs, never even considering marriage and a loving commitment to her.

Most of the women in town wouldn't give her the time of day. She was shunned in public. When she walked through town, people would avoid her and walk on the opposite side on the alley. She would feel and see judgmental glances directed at her. Her family disowned her and the man she was living with now was not her husband either. Samantha went to the well at noon because she knew she would be alone. All the other women would have drawn their water in the morning when it was cool.

Jesus responds to Samantha's sharp rebuff by saying, "First off, you have no idea who I am. If you did know who I am, you would actually want to talk with me, because I have something to offer you, a gift from God, living water."

Samantha, in a sarcastic tone, says, "You know, this well is pretty deep. And you don't have a rope and bucket to get me any of this 'living water'. (She pulls the rope and bucket towards her.) The water from this well has provided life for my ancestor Jacob, his relatives, his animals, and everyone for centuries. So I don't think you can give me any water that's better than what I already have."

Jesus looks straight at Samantha and said, "But with this water, you'll get thirsty again. The water I want to give you will take away your thirst forever. It's like having a never ending spring inside you that gives you eternal life." Skeptical, yet desiring something better than the life she has now, Samantha says, "You know, if you had water like that, I'd like to have some.

Then I wouldn't have to come out here in the hot sun to fetch water ever again."

Jesus says, "Alright, go get your husband so I can offer you this gift." Samantha closes her eyes, sighs deeply and says, "I don't have a husband." She's thinking 'Great! Here it starts again, another public embarrassment!'

Jesus without skipping a beat responds, "I know, you don't have a husband, because you've been sleeping around with five different guys. In essence you've had five husbands and you're not married to the guy you're living with now."

How freaked out would you be if a complete stranger told you intimate details about your life? Samantha freaked out. She realized that something weird and supernatural was going on. She realizes that Jesus is different but tries to avoid the personal nature of the conversation by bringing up again their cultural differences and a theological question. She says, "You may be a prophet but answer this question for me. As Samaritans we worship God here at Mt. Gerizum like our ancestors have for centuries. Why are you Jews so judgmental, saying that Jerusalem is the only true place to worship God?"

Jesus responds directly to her question, "You know a time is coming soon when it won't matter whether you worship God the Father in Jerusalem or at your mountain. But, as a Samaritan you know that the scriptures say that the Messiah will come from the Jews and not the Samaritans. What's most important for you to know is that God is looking for anyone who will truly worship him in a spirit of truth. Many people attend church to fulfill some cultural expectation or perform a meaningless religious ritual, but God desires for us to come before him with a transparent heart and mind."

This truth touches Samantha. She understands and desires the reality of this honest and revolutionary teaching from this stranger. She replies, "Yes, I know the Messiah is coming and when he does he will explain everything to us about truly loving and knowing God."

Sensing her openness, Jesus tells her, "I am the Messiah!" In a moment of spiritual revelation, Samantha stares at Jesus and asks within her heart, "Is it possible? Could this prophet be the Messiah? He knows me without ever knowing me. His words seem powerful and true. His concern for me feels real and authentic, unlike anyone I've ever known." Hoping for a new direction in her life and with the excitement that Jesus may indeed be the Messiah, Samantha rushes back into town.

She returns to the community that judges her and despises her. She returns to her community with a message of hope. Samantha's social shame and personal pain is buried under her hope for a new life through the presence and forgiveness of the Messiah. Striding through the walkways of the village she yells, "Come out to the well and meet a man who told me everything I ever did! I think he could be the Messiah!"

The disciples of Jesus return to the well with some food right when Jesus and the woman were finishing *their conversation. Feeling frustrated with being in Samaria in the first place, they think, "Why is Jesus talking to a Samaritan woman? All we need is trouble while we're traveling through God-forsaken place!"*

They go and sit with Jesus. Jesus teaches them about a coming spiritual harvest. A harvest where one person will plant spiritual seeds, and then others will actually gather the harvest. He explains it will be a harvest of people finding spiritual eternal life.

The disciples hear some noise in the distance behind them. The turn around and see to their amazement hundreds of people streaming out of Sychar towards them. The spiritual harvest is about to begin, and it was planted by the words of a woman. This spiritual awakening was started by a woman who this morning was the town slut and this afternoon is a new daughter of God.

The people of Sychar listen as Jesus teaches. This village of Samaritans begs this Jewish Rabbi to stay with them. For two days, they heard the astounding and refreshing message of God's grace and reconciliation. Many choose to believe that Jesus is indeed the promised Messiah. The people of Sychar are quoted as saying, "Now we believe because we have heard him ourselves, not just because of what you told us. He is indeed the Savior of the world."

– Jesus story paraphrased from John 4:1-42.

⌘   ⌘   ⌘

This renewal and recycling of one's life is the purpose and power found in Jesus Christ. The issues of rejecting a woman as a pastor or a teacher of men seem trivial and ludicrous when put in the context of the miracle in Samantha's life. If you would've told the people in Sychar that their lives would be changed forever through the experience of Samantha meeting the Messiah, they would have thought you were crazy! It was something they wouldn't have even considered as an option.

How about you? How crazy is it to consider Jesus being the center of your spiritual life? Would it make a difference in your life if you discovered the love and life that God desires for you through Jesus? Jesus liberated the lives of adulterous women, hateful bigots, prostitutes, arrogant academics, and everyday people who thought they had the spiritual and real life answers to their lives. It doesn't matter how detached you feel from God's love or how messed up the social situation is you're living in. A real conversation with Jesus can tear down all that crap.

To review, Jesus in this experience with the Samaritans showed his love for people and guided them to a real and relevant relationship with God, despite the obstacles of sectarian prejudice, gender discrimination, and moral and social isolation. Jesus cares, and in reality, Jesus can actually save someone from themselves and from the destructive cultural landscape that surrounds them.

Before I jump into another Jesus story, let's acknowledge how important women are to the story and message of God. For example, there were women disciples of Jesus! They were as equally important to the success of Jesus' ministry and the early church as the men were. We aren't aware of all of them, but a few of the women disciples were Mary Magdalene, Joanna, Susanna, Salome, Mary, & Martha.

⌘　⌘　⌘

Jesus Story

Once, Jesus was teaching in a synagogue on the Sabbath Day, a Saturday. He saw a woman who was crippled, bent over, and had been unable to stand up straight for eigtheen years. He touched her and instantly healed her! She stood up straight and immediately began thanking God. The religious leader at the synagogue was furious at Jesus! Why? Because Jesus had broken a religious law saying that you could not heal someone on the Sabbath day. The Sabbath was meant to be a day of rest to focus on honoring God, so no work was allowed. Healing the woman was considered "work" and thereby dishonorable to God.

Jesus told the synagogue leader how unloving he was to defend this destructive religious law and not rejoice over this woman's healing. While rebuking the religious leader for his callousness, Jesus referred to the healed woman as a "Daughter of Abraham." Men in Jewish culture were at times referred to as the "Sons of Abraham." Jesus was giving her and all women equal status with men before God and within the

religious culture of the day. This shocked the religious leaders and made them hate Jesus even more.
    – Jesus Story paraphrased from Luke 13:10-17.

⌘　⌘　⌘

Jesus' death and his resurrection changed human history. Women had pivotal roles in these events. Following is a Jesus story that caused many of the religious leaders to say in a loud voice, "Oh shit! It's Jesus, again!"

⌘　⌘　⌘

Jesus Story
Jesus was dead. He had been beaten by the fists of priests, whipped and scourged by the Roman military, and physically nailed to a cross through his wrists and feet. A huge crowd saw him die a horrible death in public. Almost all of the male disciples were hiding in fear for their lives. They were afraid of being arrested like Jesus or attacked by a mob opposing Jesus.

The religious leaders remembered that Jesus claimed he would rise from the grave in three days after his death. They posted military guards at Jesus' tomb to keep the disciples from possibly stealing his body and then claiming that Jesus had come back to life. This precaution underscored how the civic and religious leaders drastically misunderstood the reality and true nature of Jesus' mission and his followers. His followers were not in a patriotic or religious revolution against the Romans or the established church.

The disciples would never have thought of doing something as vile as grave desecration and stealing Jesus' body to fake his resurrection in an attempt to further their "cause". These men and women were the loving extended family of Jesus and this horrible thought would have never crossed their mind even though they were in a desperate state.

The faith and hopes of the Jesus Followers have been crushed. Jesus, who had physically saved others from angry mobs, the ravages of disease, and even physical death, choose not to save himself with his supernatural power. In the minds of the people, Jesus didn't have the power to save himself. It was a humiliating defeat for the power and authority that Jesus claimed he had.

In the minds of the disciples, it was over. The disciples kept mentally replaying the events of the past three years. They thought of what Jesus had taught them, and the great moments they had together helping others. Each disciple wondered silently if all the sacrifices they had made to follow Jesus had been worth it, and they wondered what to do now. It's interesting to know that the men and women disciples were not anticipating or hoping for Jesus to return to life. One reason for that may be the stark reality of the brutal death they saw Jesus go through.

Three days after Jesus' death the women who were disciples, Mary Magdalene , the other Mary- not the mother of Jesus, Salome, & Joanna, and a few others went out to visit Jesus' tomb at sunrise on Sunday. They were going to apply burial spices to Jesus' body according to their tradition. This would be somewhat similar to the modern tradition of placing flowers at someone's grave that people do today as an act to show their love and loss for the person who has died.

This early morning the women disciples followed the narrow trail to Jesus' tomb so they could apply the burial spices to his body. One of them thought out loud, "Hey, how are we going to roll back that giant rock covering the entrance to Jesus' tomb?" No one answered.

Moments earlier at Jesus' tomb the small company of soldiers assigned to guard Jesus' body were wondering how to pass the time for the third straight boring day. Their boredom soon ended. Suddenly it felt and sounded like a giant earthquake. The guards looked around and almost peed in their pants at what they saw. An Angel of the Lord was rolling the stone aside on Jesus' tomb. This entity was dressed in super bright white clothing, and his face shined in a bright white light! As the stone was rolled away and the interior of the tomb came into view, they noticed that Jesus' body was missing from the tomb!

When the Angel finished rolling away the giant stone, he flew up and sat on the top of the stone and looked down at them. The soldiers, scared to death at this supernatural event, fainted and passed out. A God directed supernatural intervention surely caused all the soldiers to go unconscious.

The women disciples approaching on the trail felt the earthquake also. One of the women more than likely blurted out "Holy shit!" Why? Two days ago another earthquake had occurred when Jesus died on the cross. They knew something supernatural had happened. They anxiously walked up to the tomb. Something strange had happened. The soldiers were lying unconscious on the ground. The tomb was open. They women were very scared and on edge.

Some of the women tenuously walked inside the tomb, while others stood outside. Jesus' body was gone, which caused them great grief and fear. What really freaked them out was that the linen wrapping that surrounded Jesus' body and his head was lying flat in the tomb. It was as if Jesus' body had just melted or vaporized, leaving the linen "deflated" exactly where his body had been. No one stealing his body could have left the linen lying in such a perfect position.

While they were looking at this weird sight, something more frightening occurred; the Angel of the Lord instantly reappeared inside the tomb. Immediately, he says, "Don't be afraid! I know you're here looking for Jesus from Nazareth who was killed (Jesus was a common name so the Angel was clarifying for certain which Jesus he was talking about). "You women who are outside, come on in. As you can see, Jesus is not here. He has been raised from the dead and is alive again just as he said he would be. Remember, he told you and others plainly that he would be betrayed, he would be executed, and he would come back to life. Run back quickly and tell Peter and the other disciples what has happened. Tell them that Jesus has been brought back to life from the dead and that he is going to meet all of you in Galilee. You will see Jesus there. Remember all this I have told you." The women were trembling in shock from this bizarre and overwhelming experience. Numb, frightened and not able to say a word, they began running back to the house where the disciples were huddled together.

The Roman soldiers regained consciousness after the women left. They woke up not knowing for sure what happened, but they quickly realized they had all been out of it for a while. They looked around, saw that Jesus' body was gone, and one shouted "Damn! We're screwed!" The Roman military leaders would have the soldiers executed for failing to guard the tomb. It would be seen as gross incompetence to allow a band of "religious zealots" to "steal the body" and continue a perceived threat to the civil order.

The soldiers knew they had a better chance of personal survival by appealing for help from the religious leaders instead of going straight to their superior officers and reporting that Jesus' body was gone. They told the religious leaders the bizarre story of the earthquake, which was probably felt by everyone in Jerusalem, and Jesus' body disappearing. In detail they described the Angel, becoming unconscious, and then waking up to find Jesus' body "vaporized" but his burial shroud still in the tomb. The religious leaders had the most to lose if Jesus was indeed resurrected from the dead. They decided to pay off the guards so they could fabricate a lie, saying that the disciples had stolen Jesus' body while the guards were sleeping.

The religious leaders would protect the soldiers from punishment by their superior officers, they needed the soldiers false story to protect their interests. The disciples would be seen as out of control zealots willing to steal a dead body to further their "insurrection" against Rome and the established religious order. This conspiracy would protect the Roman officials from a zealot uprising and protect the religious leaders' control and influence over the people.

Side Note: For Jesus' body to have been stolen by the disciples and for the religious leader's conspiracy story to be true the following would have had to occur:

- Every one of the soldiers was derelict in their duty and fell asleep at the same time while guarding the tomb
- The disciples of Jesus somehow slipped passed all the sleeping soldiers guarding the tomb
- A large stone in front of the tomb was moved by the disciples without making any noise loud enough to wake up the sleeping soldiers
- The smell of Jesus' decomposed body did not alert the sleeping soldiers that the tomb had been opened
- The dead and beaten body of Jesus was carried by the disciples past the sleeping guards without waking them up (Removing a body from a tomb goes against all Jewish

social teachings about defiling a dead body, touching a dead body, and keeping yourself "clean" before God)

- Peter, who had publicly denied Christ two days earlier, and the other male disciples that were shamed and hiding in fear for the lives, somehow decided to risk their lives by confronting Roman soldiers with swords who could easily kill them to steal Jesus' body

- Somehow the followers of Jesus, whose crucial beliefs were based on a moral life of honesty and honoring God, choose to become liars and deceivers to perpetuate a lie that would go against everything their now dead friend had taught them and show utter disrespect for Jesus' life and message.

If you desire to be intellectually honest, tolerant, and open to divergent view points, I encourage you to consider the resurrection of Jesus from the dead.

But back again to the women disciples. Mary, Joanna, Salome, Mary Magdalene, and others were running along the trail to find the other disciples so that they could tell them this great news from the Angel; the news that Jesus had come back to life after a brutal death. Suddenly and without warning, Jesus appeared on the trail and basically said, "Hey guys, how's it going?" The women were scared but at the same filled with so much joy from seeing Jesus alive! After seeing the horrible death of Jesus, they knew they were involved in a supernatural and holy experience. In an act of worship, the women fell down at Jesus' feet, held on to his feet, and praised God that he was alive.

In an encouraging voice, Jesus told them, "Don't be afraid! Go tell my other disciples to go to Galilee and they will see me there." The women stood up and hesitantly left Jesus, walking, looking back, and then running again to go tell the other disciples. The women burst into the home where the other Jesus followers were. Catching their breath from their run up the hill, they shouted, "The tomb is empty! Jesus is alive! We have seen the Lord!"

Some of the men scoffed at the women saying, "You're nuts! Why should we listen to you? Let us mourn in peace." Mary Magdalene stood her ground and forcefully pleaded, "An Angel of the Lord appeared and told us Jesus had risen. Jesus' burial cloth was lying empty in the tomb. We saw Jesus alive!! He told us to go to Galilee and wait for him there!"

Peter and John looked across the room at each other. Without saying a word, they each thought, "Could this really be happening? Maybe what Jesus taught us is actually coming true." Soon afterward, the risen Jesus appeared to all the disciples in several different places. Many not expecting to see Jesus, because he was dead, would recognize Jesus and a few probably joyfully shouted out loud, "Oh shit! It's Jesus!"

Jesus Story paraphrased from the writings of the disciples John, Matthew, and Mark.

⌘   ⌘   ⌘

How great is it that in the male dominated culture of Jesus' time, God chose to reveal the news of Jesus' rising from the dead to women first? Women were not respected enough in the Jewish culture of Jesus' time to even testify in court as a witness; the word of a woman meant nothing. Yet God chose and trusted the women disciples of Jesus to carry the news of Jesus' resurrection to the men who were also disciples. Women, not men, were the first teachers of the power and reality of Jesus as the resurrected Son of God to the doubters and skeptics in the world. It's encouraging that there are many churches and groups that celebrate and support women in leadership as pastors and spiritual teachers.

The fact that women were the first to testify that Jesus was resurrected is a powerful argument that the written scriptural accounts of the disciples are authentic and were not "manufactured" at a later date. If the Christian scriptures about Jesus were written by men many decades or centuries later in an effort to present Jesus as something he truly wasn't, to in effect lie, the men in power writing these stories would never had given such a prominent role to women and described the men as doubting cowards.

Jesus was and is the real life liberator of women. He is the spiritual liberator of everyone: men, women, children, the elderly, the depressed, the abused, the arrogant, the self-absorbed, etc. I pray and hope that if you're a woman who's been turned off to Jesus by the actions of the church, you'll give Jesus another chance. Jesus, the Son of God, desires to bring you joy, respect, and meaning in life now and for eternity!

Do Something

Reflect on and make a list of the wisdom and direction the women in your life have given you. Thank them and God for that.

Please send your critical comments, encouragements, and questions to steve@ ohshititsjesus.com. You can post your thoughts and join a discussion about the book and this chapter on www.ohshititsjesus.com and on the Facebook group "Oh Shit Its Jesus".

Chapter Nine
Las Vegas, Outer Space, Jesus & You?

Have you been to Vegas? Here is a city whose economic base is built upon the foundation of taking a person's money from them and fulfilling a person's self-centered desires. When the gamblers see the huge buildings and lights of the Las Vegas strip you would think they might ask, "Who or what pays for all this glitz?" The glaring fact that "the house always wins" is lost on them. They're handing over their money to a stranger, hoping the stranger will give them more money back. They have an against-all-odds hope, and that hope is in a lie, the lie that money will make them happy.

There was a great movie several years back about establishing contact with an intelligent extraterrestrial society. In the movie a radio astronomer is searching for extraterrestrial life and receives a coded signal from an alien civilization. The signal contains a design for a transport vehicle for one person to travel through a wormhole to this distant cosmic civilization. The United States, along with an international alliance, contributes an immense amount of funds to construct this space transport.

The radio astronomer does not believe in God or spiritual faith because she believes there is no empirical scientific evidence to support having a faith in God. Using the space transport she travels through an awe-inspiring cosmic view of galaxies, star systems, and planets. She has a meeting with a "spokesbeing" from this alien civilization. The alien entity explains to her that the most important truth their advanced society has discovered is that "We are not alone." In other words, relationships are the most important things in all life. The "spokesbeing" speaks to the astronomer in the physical form of her Dad who died when she was about twelve years old. She had a very loving relationship with her dad and misses him very much. The alien appears to her as her father to help her better understand and relate to the message of hope and desire for relationship and community.

She is zipped back home in the transport, having been gone for a period of eighteen hours. However, due to the special properties of her alien transport it appears to the mission control that her transport never left or was only gone for a microsecond. None of the video or audio devices she was carrying recorded any of her galactic views or the meeting with the alien entity.

It appears to those who didn't experience the astronomer's journey that all this time and fortune has been wasted on a meaningless project. Therefore, she is summoned to appear before a congressional panel to explain and justify her experience. She realizes that she is asking people to accept the truth and reality of her cosmic experience on faith. She's asking people to accept her experience with the kind of "spiritual faith" that she has been ridiculing throughout her life. Following is her testimony before Congress in the movie:

COMMITTEE CHAIRMAN

(Speaking to the astronomer) *You come before us with no evidence. No records, no artifacts – only a story that – to put it mildly – strains credibility. Over two trillion dollars was spent, hundreds of lives were lost, many more may be in jeopardy due to the almost incalculable worldwide psychological impact… Are you going to sit there and tell us that we should simply take this all on faith?*

CONGRESSMAN

Answer the question, Doctor. As a scientist – can you prove any of this?

ASTRONOMER

No.

CONGRESSMAN

So why don't you admit what by your own standards must be the truth: that this experience simply didn't happen.

ASTRONOMER (with tears welling up in her eyes)

Because I can't. I had… an experience. I can't prove it. I can't even explain it. All I can tell you is that everything I know as a human being, everything I am – tells me that it was real.

I was given something wonderful. Something that changed me. A vision of the universe that made it overwhelmingly clear just how tiny and insignificant – and at the same time how rare and precious we all are. A vision… that tells us we belong to something greater than ourselves… that we're not – that none of us – is alone. I wish I could share it. I wish everyone, if only for a moment – could feel that sense of awe, and humility… and hope. That continues to be my wish.

The closing statement of the astronomer parallels in many ways the experience that Followers of Christ have had with Jesus. Following is a rewrite of the astronomer's last statement from a Christ Followers perspective:

"I had a spiritual experience. I can't prove it. I can't even fully explain it. All I can tell you is that everything I know as a human being, everything I am – tells me that it was real, that Jesus is real. I was given something wonderful. Something that changed me. A vision of the universe that made it overwhelmingly clear just how tiny and insignificant – and at the same time how rare and precious we all are to God. A vision… that tells us we belong to something greater than ourselves… that we're not – that none of us – is alone. The Spirit of Jesus is with us and desires a relationship with us. I wish to share my personal connection with God to others. I wish everyone, if only for a moment – could feel that sense of awe, and humility, and hope found in Jesus. That continues to be my wish."

This is the "wish" that myself and others have for you; desiring for you to know and have a personal spiritual relationship with Jesus. The astronomer, like many today, had bought into the lie that human science and knowledge would lead to personal fulfillment and understanding. Many tourists in Las Vegas believe that self-indulgence in gambling, money, and illicit sex will bring happiness and meaning to their life. What lies have you listened to and followed hoping to "find yourself" and bring meaning to your life?

As Christ followers, we do not have all the answers we would like to have. (It's annoying when Christians and preachers think they have an answer for everything.) However, unlike the astronomer's experience, humanity does have archaeological and historical proof of Jesus, his life, and teachings from non-religious universities and research institutions.

So what about you? Concerning your life, what or whom do you place your faith in? What is that faith based on? Are your beliefs about life and the afterlife based upon what you have devised yourself or founded on a realistic faith in a more powerful and knowledgeable spiritual entity? Wouldn't you rather have a spiritual guide who is not vague, but gives a clear message, and relates to you personally?

⌘　⌘　⌘

Jesus Story

When Jesus arrived In towns, crowds would gather to hear his teachings and to possibly witness some of the miraculous events they had heard about. When he arrived at the town of Capernaum, it was like a rock star had arrived and a huge crowd surrounded him. A respected local religious leader, Jarius, pushed his way through the crowd of his friends and townspeople. He strained his head above the noisy throng looking towards the center of the crowd for this Jesus. There was a reason for Jarius' urgency. His twelve year old daughter was dying, now.

When he was finally near Jesus, he pushed his way to be in front of Jesus. There, he fell to his knees at Jesus' feet. Jarius is a respected religious leader who supposedly has all the answers and access to God's blessings. Now he is begging a "day laborer" from a small village to come save his daughter's life. He was desperate. The colleagues and friends of Jarius rejected Jesus' message and claims as God's Son, yet Jarius saw Jesus as his best option for his daughter. This would be somewhat similar to a pastor of a large city church going to a homeless wandering religious teacher, recognizing his superior knowledge, acknowledging his special relationship to God, and begging for his help.

Jesus picked Jarius up off the dirt and said, "Let's go see your daughter." Jarius' heart now became hopeful even though he was still anxiously scared for his daughter. Leading Jesus through this crowd, Jarius picked up his pace and walked briskly toward his *house; his daughter's life was at stake. As they were walking, all of a sudden Jesus stopped and asked, "Who touched me?" Peter says, "What? Everyone in this crowd is bumping up against you." Jesus quickly replies, "No, not that! Someone purposely touched me with a seeking heart. I felt the healing power of God go out from me." As Jesus spoke, he turned his head around, scanning the crowd around him to discover who had touched him.*

A woman in the crowd for the past twelve years had a form of hemophilia, possibly a debilitating menstrual bleeding disorder. She became afflicted with the problem the same year Jarius' daughter was born. She suffered as an outcast in her own community. Her family was embarrassed and felt shamed because a woman who was menstruating was considered "unclean" by religious tradition. Therefore, she was considered to be unacceptable to be in the presence of God and forbidden to offer any sacrifice or prayers to God. Anyone who touched her or was in her presence was considered "unclean" and thereby unacceptable to be with God. Unnoticed by the crowd, she worked her way through them thinking, "If I can just touch Jesus' robe, I'll be healed!" She had faith and belief in Jesus as the Son of God and therefore believed in the healing power and authority he had within him.

The crowd stopped, wondering what was going on. Anxious to have Jesus come save his daughter's life, Jarius thought, "What's happening? Why have we stopped?" The woman who reached out to Jesus realized she would soon be discovered and identified by her fellow townspeople. She stepped forward and fell down in reverence at Jesus' feet. She quickly explained her illness and that she was the one who touched his robe, knowing that if she only touched him, she would be healed. She explained her struggle to Jesus, Jarius and the crowd. The woman had spent all her hard earned money on doctors but her condition only became worse. Now she joyously shared that immediately after touching Jesus' robe she felt the power of God heal her. Her bleeding had stopped!

According to the local tradition, a religious teacher wearing his robe is only allowed to be touched by his family in public. The crowd knew this. Each person did not want to be the cause for this delay in saving Jarius' daughter. Everyone was relieved when the woman came forward with her story because they had been bumping up against and touching Jesus' robe.

Jesus reached down to the woman; He helped her to stand up and said, "Daughter, your faith has made you well. Go in peace. You have been healed." As Jesus was saying this, a couple of Jarius' friends ran up and told him, "Jarius, I'm so sorry, but your daughter is dead. There's no need for Jesus now." This sad news spread through the crowd. Jarius' grief and sadness was crushing. His grief was magnified thinking of the "Ifs." "If only I had found Jesus earlier." "If the woman had not delayed us, my daughter may still be alive."

The woman who was healed experienced in the span of a minute, both the joy of being restored to health and the fear of being blamed for delaying Jesus *and indirectly causing the death of Jarius' daughter. You have two people, Jarius and the woman, who were initially hopeful, but then experienced dread and sadness again. Jesus, in the center of this heavy sadness and shock turned to Jarius, placed a hand on his shoulder and said, "Don't be afraid. Just trust me."*

Jesus and the crowd then followed Jarius to his home. The woman who was healed follows along at the back of the crowd. As they approached the house, they heard the sounds of grief and wailing echo down the dirt street; the family's crying and sorrowful anguish was spilling out of the open windows. Jarius went inside. Jesus motioned to Peter, James, and John to come with him into the house. The disheartened crowd stayed outside the house.

The scene inside Jarius' home was one Jesus and the disciples knew well. The death of a child was not an uncommon experience during these ancient times. They all had been in the homes of friends and family when a child had died and personally shared in the grief. Unexpected, Jesus said something that seemed immensely callous and insensitive; he said "Why all this weeping and commotion? The child is not dead; she is only sleeping." With shock and some anger the people in the house began laughing at and mocking Jesus. They knew the girl was dead. They had seen her! How dare he be so cruel to say that she is only sleeping?

When everyone's laughter and insults died down, Jesus looked over at Jarius and his wife, then turned to the family and friends in the room and said, "I want you all to go outside, leave." They looked towards Jarius; he slightly nodded and motioned with his hand for them to leave. The family and friends respectfully filed out of the room with confused looks on their faces. Without asking, Jesus walked into the room where the twelve-year-old girl lay dead. Jarius and his wife followed along with the three disciples.

In great contrast to a few minutes ago, the house and the crowd outside were now silent. Jesus knelt down and tenderly held the girl's hand. Outside in the courtyard the crowd heard Jesus in a loud but kind voice say, "Get up little girl!" Instantly, with the vibrancy of life, the girl sat-up and jumps to her feet. Her mother rushed to her daughter and fell to her knees crying tears now of joy and squeezed the girl in a hug. She ran her hands over the girl's face, staring at her to be reassured that her daughter who was cold and dead only moments ago was now alive and walking around! Jarius, overwhelmed with this miracle of life and feeling the relief that only a parent can know wrapped his arms around his wife and daughter. Jesus stepped back and said, "You know she's been sick for awhile. You need to give her something to eat." That's a dinner the family never forgot.

Outside the family and friends heard the shouts of joy from the girl's mom. Jesus and the three disciples walked outside through the front door. The crowd rushed back inside the house to witness the miracle of restored life and hope. There was no more laughing or mocking directed towards Jesus from the crowd outside or inside the house. The people, in true awe, talked to each other in hushed words about how this man Jesus has the power over life and death.

As Jesus and the disciples left the house they walked past by the woman who had been healed earlier. For the second time in one day, Jesus had saved her life from despair and anguish. Years later, when this woman would see the girl who was brought back to life, now a young woman, she remembered the salvation and life Jesus had brought to both their lives.

– Jesus story paraphrased from Luke 8:40-56; Mark 5:21-43.

⌘ ⌘ ⌘

I hate to break this to you, but you are not a divine creature, you are not God. What gives you the right to believe that you have the power to determine if you spend an eternity in the afterlife with a divine God? Wouldn't that be the divine spiritual entity's decision not yours? God asks that you admit you're a screw-up and to seek him out. How silly is it to think that by performing some religious ritual, burning some incense, or having enough good karma you can obtain the right or power to be with God in the afterlife? I hope you give this some serious thought and reflection later.

Do Something

1) How about giving Jesus another chance or a first look? He may actually be who he

says he is. How would that change your life?

2) Giving to a charity is great. However, how about actually becoming a volunteer once a month, through an annual event, or, whenever? Take a look at how God can use you to be a positive force for good in someone's life.

3) Do you desire a relationship with Jesus? Do you have the faith to believe that Jesus is God's Son? Do you believe that Jesus can bring meaning to your life now and in the afterlife? If so, reach out to God. Call out to God. Pray. Tell God that you know he loves you and ask him to forgive you for all the crap in your life. Ask God to be part of your life. Ask God to help your journey in life. Tell God that you desire to follow the love and teachings of Jesus. If you choose to do so, Jesus promises to journey with you, and God promises to give you eternal life.

4) If you are seeking God, I encourage you to find a group of Christ Followers and share with them your journey with God. Look for ways to build supportive friendships within this group and partner with them in helping their community and others.

Please send your critical comments, encouragements, and questions to steve@ohshititsjesus.com. You can post your thoughts and join a discussion about the book and this chapter on www.ohshititsjesus.com and on the Facebook group "Oh Shit Its Jesus".

Acknowledgements

I was finally convinced to write this book by my friends in the 2006 Yosemite Tribe of Jesus. Thanks for telling me to get to off my butt and write this stuff down.

Thanks to all my friends and ministry assistants who dialogued with me about spiritual and life issues while driving in Yosemite or hiking on a trail. I wish I could list you all, but you know who you are. God used much of your wisdom, affirmations, and counsel in the writing of this book.

I need to give a thanks to my wife Karen and friends Lauren and Ryan for their input on the content of the book.

A special thanks to Amber Parker! She was a grammatical and spiritual editor for the book. She spent numerous hours providing proofreading and editorial advice. (Thanks Ethan for allowing her to spend time on this!)

Thanks to my wife Karen, son Chad, daughter-in-law Liza, and my son Josh for their encouragement and love.

Thanks to the churches, my supervisors, family members, and individuals who have supported and given me the opportunity to be a minister at Yosemite.

Index of Jesus Stories

Chapter 1
  I Know Other Christians, but You're Different
  Luke 7:36-50.
  Jesus forgives a sinful woman at the religious leader Simon's house.

Chapter 2
  Street Preachers, Jesus Freaks, Bible Thumpers, and other Annoying People
  John 2:13-22.
  Jesus using his authority as God on earth, clears the merchants and animals defiling the worship area in the Temple known as the Court of the Gentiles.

Chapter 3
  I Don't Want to Be a Christian
  Matthew 16
  After performing fantastic supernatural miracles, Jesus is upset by the lack of faith the religious leaders of the day and even his own disciples have in him.

Chapter 4
  There's Nothing Holy About This Book – the Bible
  Passage referenced. Hebrews 4:12-13.
  John 1:1-14.

One of the original followers of Jesus, John writes about Jesus being God, the creator of the Universe, in human form. He explains because of God's love for us, even though we reject God's purpose in our lives, he gives us the chance for a new spiritual life through faith in Jesus.

Chapter 5
What the Hell?
Luke 16:1-31. Jesus tells a story about a selfish rich man who after his death tries to bargain with God in the afterlife.

Chapter 6
Dark Matter, Dinosaurs, Darwin, and Dark Chocolate
Matthew 9:1-8. Jesus astounds the religious leaders and people of a community when he forgives a paralyzed man's sin and then heals him so he can walk again.

Chapter 7
The Church Sucks
Matthew 22:34-40.
Jesus is asked by religious skeptics what is the most important commandment that God gave to Moses we should follow.

Chapter 8
Jesus, Liberator of Women and Social Revolutionary

Luke 10:38-42.

Jesus allows one of his female disciples, Mary, to violate a social taboo by listening to him teaching while sitting up front amongst men in the same room.

John 4:1-42.

Shattering a few cultural barriers, Jesus restores a woman and many in a village to a real and relevant relationship with God by ignoring historical and cultural prejudices.

Luke 13:10-17.

Jesus violates an idiotic man-made religious law and heals a crippled woman and teaches that God sees women and men equally as His children.

Compiled from the writings of the disciples John, Matthew, and Mark.

The events surrounding Jesus' resurrection teach that God reveals and trusts the message of Jesus' miraculous rising from the dead and being alive to the women disciples first.

Chapter 9

Las Vegas, Outer Space, Jesus and You
Luke 8:40-56; Mark 5:21-43.

A woman is healed by Jesus of a debilitating bleeding disorder and brings a twelve year-old girl back to life after she dies. These miracles occur because of the unwavering faith that the woman and the father of the girl show in Jesus as their only hope for restored life.

1103271

Made in the USA